E. Raymond Watker.
Peterhead 1962.

ETHICS AND THE GOSPEL

Ethics
AND THE GOSPEL

✦

T. W. MANSON

SCM PRESS LTD
BLOOMSBURY STREET LONDON

FIRST PUBLISHED 1960

© SGM PRESS LTD 1960

PRINTED IN GREAT BRITAIN BY

WESTERN PRINTING SERVICES LTD

BRISTOL

CONTENTS

Publisher's Note		7
Introduction by RONALD PRESTON		9
I	The Old Testament Background	11
II	Judaism and the Law of Moses	28
III	Jesus and the Law of Moses	43
IV	The Foundation of Christian Ethics: Following Christ	58
V	The Earliest Christian Community	69
VI	The Original Teaching of Jesus and the Ethics of the Early Church	87
	Index of Biblical References	105
	General Index	107

T. W. MANSON

was born in 1893 and died in 1958. Educated at Tyne-mouth High School and at the Universities of Glasgow and Cambridge, he was a minister, and in 1953 Moderator of the General Assembly, of the Presbyterian Church of England. He was Yates Professor of New Testament Greek and Exegesis at Mansfield College, Oxford, from 1932 to 1936, when he was appointed Rylands Professor of Biblical Criticism and Exegesis in the University of Man-chester. He was a Doctor of Divinity of the Universities of Cambridge, Dublin, Durham and Glasgow. Among his many publications may be mentioned *The Sayings of Jesus*. When he died, many students of the New Testament mourned a teacher who embodied what he taught.

INTRODUCTION

The six chapters of this book were originally given as an Extra-Mural evening course of lectures in Manchester University in the winter of 1952–3. They were repeated later in 1953, in substantially the same form, as the Ayer Lectures at Colgate-Rochester Divinity School in the United States of America. In the case of the first four lectures Professor Manson had prepared a fairly full manuscript; in the case of the last two he had assembled little more than a synopsis. Five of the lectures were taken down at Manchester as they were delivered. The first three follow the manuscript fairly closely, but there is some expansion and the style is more popular and, indeed, racy in places. The typescript of the fifth and sixth is of course a great expansion of the scanty notes. The fourth lecture was apparently not taken down verbatim (the typescript merely follows the manuscript); that is why it is shorter than the others, for there is no record of the way in which Professor Manson expanded his manuscript in giving the lecture.

Professor Manson had begun the revision of the first lecture for publication and the first few pages of the second. His revision chiefly took the form of adding a number of references, re-writing colloquial passages and removing allusions to passing events. The process of preparing these

lectures for publication has therefore consisted in con-
tinuing the revision along the same lines. Professor
Manson did not work by a series of provisional manu-
scripts; what he prepared he did slowly and with great
care. There is, therefore, scarcely any doubt what he
wished to say.

The Biblical passages in the text of the lectures are
given exactly as Professor Manson spoke them; some
are probably from the new English version of the New
Testament due to be published in 1961 (drafts of which
he was in the habit of using in lectures), some may
be his own translations, and some are from the existing
English versions.

The work of checking Biblical references was begun
under the direction of Professor Matthew Black of St
Andrews, who is Professor Manson's literary executor, by
the Revd Alan Quigley, now of Dunedin, New Zealand.
It was completed in Manchester by Mr J.W. Rogerson,
a student of the Faculty of Theology and of St Anselm
Hall, who also undertook most of the checking and searching out of other references.

RONALD PRESTON

St Anselm Hall
University of Manchester

one

THE OLD TESTAMENT
BACKGROUND

IT is possible to begin discussions about ethics along various lines. One of them is the philosophical. Here we begin by recognizing that there is a certain area of human experience which can be called the moral or the ethical field, and that when people start to talk of it they naturally tend to use a number of technical terms like 'good' and 'bad', 'ought' and 'ought not', 'conscience', 'duty' and so on. Then we can set to work by making a careful examination of the technical terms and trying to ascertain exactly what they mean; and go on from that to study different codes of morality and to discuss such questions as whether there is such a thing as an absolute ethical code. Or if we do not care to do that, we can ask ourselves whether there is any general formula which will express what we mean when we talk about things being good and bad. We can, for example, define 'good' as the greatest happiness of the greatest number.

I am not going to attempt anything like this. I propose to begin in a strictly empirical way, and to put before you a survey of the teaching about morality which the Bible offers to anyone who wishes to go into the matter and to know more about it. Let us begin at the beginning, with the Old Testament background. We will take as the starting point of our study a very simple fact, with which most of us are by now quite familiar. Whenever there is a project of some kind of social change, for example the provision of better houses for the masses, almost certainly two voices will be heard in the discussion. One says that the only way to make the slum-dweller better is to remove him from his present environment and put him into better surroundings. It is urged that if you do that and give him a fair chance in a better house with proper amenities and pleasant surroundings, he will adapt himself to his new environment and become a respectable citizen. The other voice, less hopeful, says that if you put the slum-dweller into a better environment before very long he will be storing an extra coal supply in the bath and cutting up the banisters for firewood; and in a few months he will have brought his new house down to the level of the property which he has just left. One party or group says: 'If you want people to live better, you must improve their living conditions'; the other says: 'If you want to improve conditions, you must have better people.' I mention this not in order to adjudicate between these two points of view: it is in fact impossible to do so. You can go and take a look at the average housing estate and you will find parts of it in perfectly good order, while others reflect slum conditions. I mention the fact because it seems to reflect another fact, that our ethical ideas go back to two ways of tackling the problem of living, the Greek and the Hebrew.

For the understanding of the Greek approach it is important to remember that in the great classical expositions of the subject given by Plato and Aristotle, ethics and politics are not two separate sciences but two inseparable parts of a single discipline. That is a point made long ago by John

Burnet.[1] Plato's *Republic* takes it for granted that the basic problems of personal behaviour and those of communal organization are essentially the same problems. The only real difference is that personal behaviour is on a small scale, while communal behaviour is on a large scale. Aristotle's *Ethics* and *Politics* are published as separate books but, as Burnet showed, they are really parts I and II of the same philosophical enquiry and complementary to one another. In this way of tackling the problem the chief questions to ask are (1) what is the essential nature of the good life for man? and (2) under what social and political conditions can this good life be realized? It is as simple and practical as that. First define what you mean by the good life, and secondly discover how it is attainable. It is understood that you can, by clear thinking, define the goal, and by appro-priate action, get the conditions right. The conditions, of course, include a great variety of things, of which the most important is an elaborate educational system. If the con-ditions are satisfied, people will achieve the good life; or if they cannot achieve all of it, they will at least achieve as much as lies within their several capacities. Plato's *Republic* has no idea that all men are free and equal: in fact no Greek ideal state is based on the idea that men are equal. Every Greek state, real or ideal, depends for its economic existence

[1] *The Ethics of Aristotle*. Introd., pp. xxiv–xxxi, esp. p. xxvii. 'The *Ethics* asks the question "How is the Good for Man realized?" and the answer it gives is that legislation is the means of producing character, and that upon character depends the possibility of that activity which consti-tutes Happiness or the Good for Man. The *Politics* takes up the inquiry at this point and discusses everything connected with legislation and the constitution of the state. The whole forms one πραγματεία [*pragmateia*] or μέθοδος [*methodos*] and there is no word anywhere of ἠθική [*ethikē*] as a separate branch of study.'

in the first place on slavery, and Plato's ideal republic is one of the most sharply defined class societies that was ever invented. The rigid class system runs through it from top to bottom, and it is recognized that within that large society only a very small minority will ever attain the good life in its completeness and perfection. The classes that rank below the philosopher-kings will have a relatively good life; they will do the tasks that lie within their capacity and enjoy such pleasures as are available to them. The defenders of the community will have a satisfying military career; the workers will do their appointed jobs; and in that elaborate system of grading each class will do the task for which it is best fitted and receive a satisfying recompense. At the bottom of the social scale the worker, freeman or slave, can expect but little; at the top the philosopher-king may approach a really full and satisfying life—by Platonic standards; while in between there can be very varying degrees of competence and achievement. It seems to me, looking back on it, that the Greek way is a thoroughly scientific and completely unsentimental way of dealing with the question of individual morality and social organization. No sympathy is wasted on the underdogs; their job is to hew wood and draw water that the system may work efficiently. There is no attempt to assert the principles of liberty, equality, and fraternity. There is no declaration of the infinite value of the individual human soul.

When we turn from the great philosophers of Greece to the great prophets of Israel, we are at once struck by the difference of temper, attitude and approach to the problems of human life. The difference goes very wide and very deep and it is important that we should try to define it as clearly and accurately as we can.

First let us consider the relation between man and society, between the individual and the national or racial or social group to which he belongs. For this purpose we may take, on the one side, the attitude of the Athenian citizen to Athens and compare it with the attitude of the Israelite to Israel. What was it that made the Athenian prize his Athenian citizenship above all earthly goods? I cannot help thinking that, more than anything else, it was the fact that the brilliant culture and civilization of Athens belonged to him. As a citizen he shared in the ownership of the masterpieces of Greek art and architecture, master-pieces which even in ruin still capture the imagination and make us wish we could see them as they once were. The Athenian citizen knew and loved them: they were his, he helped protect them as a soldier in the citizen army; and as a member of the citizen body he had a voice and vote in the maintenance and control of the political system in which they had been produced. He was consciously proud of his membership of a cultured and civilized society and he was complacently contemptuous of the 'Barbarians', who had no such background to their rough and unmannerly life. He was keenly interested in the intricate mechanics of the running of a city-state, and jealously restricted the right to share in the job. More than that, of course, the city-state was a relatively small and manageable concern. It is very difficult for us to appreciate that a city-state, governing an area which in England would come under one of the smaller county councils, could have the power of life and death; power to declare war and make peace; power to do all the things which in our case are done by the Queen's ministers and the Houses of Parliament. And all this power lay in the hands of a relatively small group in which everybody knew everybody else and in which rights and privileges were very jealously guarded.

The Israelite's attitude to Israel is different. The outstanding feature in it is the intense awareness of corporate solidarity. The members of a clan or tribe in Israel feel themselves as parts of a single living whole. The kind of thing that is involved is expressed in the Book of Hosea (2.21–23): 'And in that day, says the Lord, I will answer the heavens, and they shall answer the earth; and the earth shall answer the grain, the wine, and the oil; and they shall answer Jezreel. And I will sow him for myself in the land. And I will have pity on Not pitied; and I will say to Not my people, "You are my people"; and he shall say "Thou art my God".' This refers back to the first chapter of the book, where the prophet has children: first a boy named Jezreel (1.4); then a daughter who, by God's command, is called Lo-ruhamah, meaning 'Not pitied' (1.6); the third child is a boy who has to be called Lo-'ammi, 'Not my people' because God has disowned Israel as his people (1.9). I am not at all sure that 'Not pitied' is the right translation for the girl's name; I think that what is really involved in both cases is the presence or absence of kin-feeling between God and Israel. It really means 'They are no relation of mine, no people of mine'. It is the reversal of recognition, and it goes back to the normal formula for claiming relationship in the semitic world. If you wanted to claim relationship with someone else you said, 'I am bone of your bone and flesh of your flesh'.[1] If your claim was admitted, the answer was 'Yes, you are bone of our bone and flesh of our flesh'. What is claimed and recognized is that you and the others are all part of one living

[1] Cf. Genesis 2.23; 29.14; Judges 9.2f; II Samuel 5.1.

organism. It is very difficult for us to understand this because we are accustomed to thinking of ourselves as individuals, and very much individuals. It is extremely hard to
think ourselves to the point of view where everyone within
the tribe or clan is part of 'one flesh'; where if one member
of the tribe is wounded or killed the tribe says not 'So-and-
so's blood has been spilt' but '*Our* blood has been spilt'.
That intensity of feeling for corporate solidarity has to be
kept in mind continually. It comes out in a very striking
way in Romans 11.14 where Paul speaks of stirring up 'his
flesh' to jealousy, and it is quite clear that 'his flesh' means
his fellow-countrymen, the Jewish people. It underlies his
whole teaching about the Body of Christ.

The difference between the Greek and Hebrew ways of
thinking may be expressed in this way. One Athenian
regards another Athenian as 'fellow-citizen': they are citi-
zens together of the same city. In Hebrew I do not think
there is any term corresponding to fellow-citizen.[1] If one
Hebrew wanted to express relationship to another Hebrew
he had two terms at his disposal, first $r\bar{e}^{\cdot}a$ meaning 'neighbour', and second '$\bar{a}h$ meaning 'brother', and which of
them he used depended on circumstances. The normal
thing in Hebrew usage was to say 'neighbour' if the idea
was uppermost of being members of the same nation by
physical descent, 'brother' if the emphasis was on the sharing of a common religious faith and loyalty. 'Brother' is the
term of relationship when you are thinking of the group in
its religious capacity; 'neighbour' when you are thinking
of it in its political and economic capacity.

[1] *Sunpolitēs* is not used in the Septuagint, and *politēs* is not common.
In the seven places where it can be compared with a Hebrew original, in
one it represents the Hebrew *ben-'amîm*, in another '*amith* (fellow, associate, relation), and in the remaining five $r\bar{e}^{\cdot}a$ (neighbour).

That brings us to a further point, the relation between God and Israel. The Greek ethic is concerned with the relation of the individual and the community to certain discussible and definable ideas and ideals: the Hebrew with the relation of the individual and the community to the will of a personal God. In Hebrew ethics the governing factor is the relation of human persons to a Divine Person; and that means that the good is not so much the object of philosophical enquiry as the content of divine revelation. '*He has shown* thee, O man, what is good; and what doth *the Lord require* of thee but to do justly and to love mercy and to walk humbly with thy God?' (Micah 6.8). The emphasis is on God and the things revealed by him; it is a matter of acceptance and obedience. The relation between God and the single living corporate body called Israel is a covenant relation. The terms of the covenant are the commands given and the promises made by God. If Israel will do God's will, then he will be their God and they will be his people. This covenant, with its provisions of commands and promises, is the charter of Israel's existence as the Chosen People of God. The promises are the never-failing source of the national hope and confidence: the commandments are the ever-present challenge to the conscience of the nation as a whole and of every member in particular. *And the important thing is that the commands, no less than the promises, are the gift of God to his people.*

We can now take a further step. Granted that both the commands and promises are a gift from God to Israel, we may add that they are a gift in which God reveals himself; he gives a glimpse of his own nature to his people. This is expressed by a formula that keeps on recurring in the Jewish Law: 'Ye shall be holy, for I Yahweh your God am holy.' That is the ultimate ground of Hebrew ethics: 'You must be holy because Yahweh your God is holy.'[1] We must constantly bear in mind that for the ancient Hebrew what we call the moral imperative came as a revelation of God and was, by that very fact, a call to the imitation of God. 'You are to be holy as I am holy.' This principle runs right through the Bible, till in the Gospel we find Jesus saying 'Be ye perfect, as your heavenly Father is perfect' (Matthew 5.48), 'Be ye merciful, as your Father is merciful' (Luke 6.36), and so on. The last ground of moral obligation is the command of God; and the supreme ideal is the imitation of a God who is at once king and father, who exhibits in the field of nature and history, and above all in his dealings with Israel, the qualities of holiness and righteousness, mercy and faithfulness, love and covenant-loyalty, which are to be the pattern for the behaviour of his subjects and children. It is extremely significant in this connexion that the promulgation of the specific laws which go to make up the Old Testament code of conduct is closely and constantly bound up with the record of what God has done for Israel. Regularly when God lays some specific obligation on them, it is prefaced by what he on his part has done for them; and so God's action becomes the standard and pattern on which they are to model themselves. The Ten Commandments begin not with a commandment, but with a statement: 'I am Yahweh thy God who brought thee out of the land of Egypt, out of the house of bondage' (Exodus 20.2). The code of Deuteronomy is preceded by a detailed history running to four chapters and telling of the marvellous way in which God has led Israel,

[1] Cf. Leviticus 11.44 f., 19.2, 20.7, 26; Numbers 15.40 f.; Psalm 16.3, 34.10 (in Hebrew); Daniel 8.24.

from the beginning up to that day. The first three chapters of Deuteronomy give a resumé of the events from the time when the Hebrews left the neighbourhood of Horeb-Sinai until they were on the point of beginning the invasion of the Promised Land. It is made clear that throughout this period the guiding and controlling hand has been God's. It is this fact that justifies the call in Deuteronomy 4 for unswerving loyalty to God and willing obedience to his Law. Only after all this do we come to the actual promulgation of laws and Moses says 'Hear, O Israel, the statutes and ordinances which I speak in your hearing this day, and you shall learn them and be careful to do them' (5.1), and we come to the Deuteronomic form of the Ten Commandments. In the next chapter we reach what has become a central principle of Judaism, the binding together of command and promise: 'Hear, O Israel, and observe to do it; that it may be well with thee, and that ye may increase mightily, as the Lord, the God of thy fathers, hath promised unto thee, in a land flowing with milk and honey' (6.3). But these present duties and future hopes are not set out until it is first stated what God has done for his people in the past. Again, if we take the Pentateuch as a whole, we find that the entire body of the legislation, with its 613 specific commandments (248 positive and 365 prohibitive), is set in a framework of narrative which rehearses the mighty acts of God from the beginning of the Creation down to the eve of Israel's entry into the Promised Land.

This setting of God's requirements in the framework of God's gifts is a phenomenon that constantly recurs in the Bible. It appears in the New Testament and most clearly in the Epistles, where the account of the mighty acts of deliverance wrought by God in Christ is put first and is the prelude to the demands of Christian conduct. See, for example, Romans, Galatians, Ephesians, I Peter. The first eight chapters of Romans deal with the work of salvation which God has accomplished in Christ. In chapters 9 to 11 we have the application of what has been expounded in 1-8 to the special and difficult problem created by the Jewish rejection of their Messiah. Then, when the nature and purpose of God's saving work have been fully and clearly set out, we come (12.1-15.3) to what it expected in the conduct of those who have received God's great gift. The same thing occurs in Galatians, where Paul spends four chapters explaining the inner meaning of the work of Christ and then goes on in the fifth chapter to say something about the nature of Christian freedom. Then, at the end of chapter 5 and the beginning of chapter 6 we have some plain instructions about ways of Christian living, but not before the fact and the quality of God's gift have been established. The same thing also occurs in Ephesians, exposition of divine goodness (1-3); exhortation to Christian living (4-6), and in I Peter, where the work of the Saviour is described in 1.1-2.10, and the duties of the saved in 2.11-5.11.

The importance of all this lies in the fact that it brings us face to face with the essential relation between the kingship of God and the ethical teaching of the Old Testament. In order to have a clearer appreciation of this we must look for a moment at some of the characteristic qualities of Semitic kingship. For this purpose it is useful to consider not only the works of scholarship dealing with the subject, but also the reports of men and women in modern times who have lived and worked among Semitic peoples, particularly among the Bedouin tribes of Arabia. Among the works of scholarship one thinks, for example, of Robertson Smith's *The Religion of the Semites* (with S. A. Cook's additional notes), and Pedersen's *Israel*. One can learn an immense amount from these works of scholarship; but in a different way a vast amount of illumination can be gained from Doughty's *Arabia Deserta*, or Lawrence's *Seven Pillars of Wisdom*, or the works of Miss Freya Stark and other modern writers. In some respects the most helpful works of all are those which deal specifically with the exploits of such men as Feisal and Ibn Saud. Here we can see directly what Semitic peoples look for in a king, what are the qualities in the ruler which alone will command the loyalty and obedience of the people. They can be brought under three main heads.

The first is personal courage and military skill. One of the recurrent themes of Lawrence's *Seven Pillars of Wisdom* is the immense difficulty of organizing the Arab tribesmen into military formations, and of keeping them together as a fighting force for any length of time. Almost the only thing that will do this is the personal prestige and force of character of some individual who stands unmistakably head and shoulders above his fellows in military skill and personal courage. The tribesmen will follow a leader who really leads, who can endure all the hardships that they endure, and more; who will face all the dangers that they face, and more; who knows what he means to do and is not to be cajoled or driven from his chosen path. It is of the essence of the matter that the commander is not a remote military potentate issuing orders from a GHQ away behind the lines. He is in the battle-line in person. In the thick of the fray he is the rallying-point for his men, and if he falters or fails his army will just melt away. In all this there is little difference between the Arabs in the twentieth century A.D. and the Hebrews in the eleventh or the second century B.C. A Saul or a David or a group of Maccabean brothers could rally the people and by winning victories win a throne. But equally any failure or defeat quickly brought the cry, 'To your tents, O Israel!' (I Kings 12.16).

The second special responsibility of kingship among Semitic peoples is the administration of justice. This takes place in public, and that means under the unwinking gaze of a vigilant and highly critical crowd. The king must be able to do two things superlatively well. He must master the great and growing mass of laws, customs and traditions and be able to find and apply the appropriate one in any given case. And he must have all this at his finger-tips ready for use at short notice. So far as I can discover Semitic legal procedure had little room for the reserved judgment. The good judge sees the real issues in the case and gives the right decision on the spot. Not only must he have the knowledge of the law and the ability to apply it; he must also have that peculiar genius that can leap to a fair decision where there is no guidance to be got from the existing law. He must know and apply law; and, if need be, he must make it. In that connexion we may recall the case of the two mothers claiming the one child and Solomon's decision on the matter (I Kings 3.16–27). That is the kind of judgment that never fails to impress Semitic people. The king must be able to say authoritatively what is 'done' or 'not done' in Israel; and he must be able to create new and acceptable rules and precedents to guide future generations. Swift nemesis waits on any failure to carry out that function. One recalls the account, in II Samuel 15.1–4, of the propaganda campaign preceding Absalom's revolt. Absalom is able to say to the litigants, 'See, your claims are good and right; but there is no man deputed by the king to hear you.' It may be questioned whether Absalom could have won over as many people as he did if his father had not been getting a little past full efficiency in his judicial func- tions. It is no accident that the same root *shāphat* covers both the executive and the judicial activities; and that the men whom the Old Testament calls *shōphĕtîm*, judges, were also national heroes and rulers of the people.[1]

The third royal activity is connected with worship. In modern travellers' accounts we can read of Arabian kings like Ibn Saud conducting prayers and giving religious addresses. We can find some parallels to this in the history of the Hebrew monarchy, for example Solomon's prayer at the dedication of the Temple, which he had built and furnished (I Kings 8.22–53). And, of course, there is the very striking case of the Hasmonean dynasty, who com- bined the offices of High-priest and king.

The ruler may thus be said to stand for the people in face of their enemies, to drive away dangers from outside, and in face of wrong doers within to purify the community from injustice and oppression. He also represents his people before God. At every turn he is intimately bound up with them; and his right to continue in office is closely related to the efficiency with which he discharges his royal tasks. The acid test of the monarchy is the adequacy of the king to meet the needs of his people for security: to give them free- dom from fear, freedom from injustice, and freedom to

[1] Cf. the constitution of the great Tyrian colony of Carthage in N. Africa, founded about the end of the ninth century B.C. Here the chief magistrates (judicial and executive) were the two *shōphĕtîm* (Latin *suffetes*). The word is the same as that used for the 'Judges' in Israel.

worship. This is summed up in the New Testament in the *Benedictus*, where the crowning mercy for Israel under the Messianic King is 'that we, being delivered from the power of our enemies, and free from fear should serve him (God) in holiness and righteousness, remaining in his presence all our life long' (Luke 1.74 ff.).

The ruler who conscientiously and efficiently discharges these duties is in a very real sense God's agent. He can be thought of as God's gift to his people, specially raised up by God to realize God's good purposes for Israel, and to lead them in ways that God will approve (cf. *Psalms of Solomon* 17). Within the limits set by human frailty and fallibility and the shortness of human life the good king does what God does on the grand scale. But no king, however good and efficient he may be as a king, can ever be more than God's agent. God remains the principal; and, in the Old Testament, the measure of a man's adequacy as king is the depth of his loyalty to God and the faithfulness with which he follows God's guidance. The divine verdict on a good king runs like this: 'My servant David, who kept my commandments, and who followed me with all his heart, to do that only which was right in mine eyes' (I Kings 14.8) or this: 'Josiah . . . did that which was right in the sight of the Lord, and walked in the way of David his father, and turned not aside to the right hand or to the left' (II Kings 22.2). By the same token the bad king is thus described: 'Manasseh . . . did that which was evil in the sight of the Lord, after the abominations of the heathen, whom the Lord cast out before the children of Israel . . . And Manasseh seduced them (Israel) to do more evil than did the nations whom the Lord destroyed before the children of Israel' (II Kings 21.2, 9).

We have gone quite a long way without saying anything about what is commonly regarded as the mainspring of Hebrew religion and ethics, the ideals of the Hebrew prophets. I am not going to say much about prophetic ideals because I think that we are apt to misunderstand the prophets if we think of them as setting ethical ideals before their contemporaries. We shall be much nearer the truth if we think of them as the messengers of God to Israel, and in particular to the rulers of Israel. When we look at the great prophets of the period from the rise of Saul to the downfall of the last king of Judah, we cannot but be struck by the extent to which their concern is with the concrete practical issues that confront successive rulers. Time and again the prophet comes on the scene to announce the divine decision about the course of events in the immediate future, a decision that calls for immediate action by the ruler. Or again the prophet comes to pass judgment in the name of God on some act of the king, whether in his public policy or his private life. As two examples out of very many we may take David's census of the people (II Samuel 24) and his treatment of Uriah the Hittite (II Samuel 11–12).

It has been suggested by Wheeler Robinson,[1] and the suggestion has much to commend it, that the Hebrew prophet normally speaks as one who has been allowed to attend the private Council of God. That is to say, when he uses the formula, 'Thus saith the Lord' or 'It is an oracle of the Lord' he is in effect promulgating a divine decree. The most striking example of this is the famous case of Micaiah ben Imlah in I Kings 22. Some of these decrees are concerned with the divine control of history, some with the

[1] Wheeler Robinson, *Redemption and Revelation*, pp. 138 ff.; *Inspiration and Revelation in the Old Testament*, pp. 167 ff.

divine standards of righteousness. In the latter case, what happens is that the prophet formulates in God's name a demand for certain kinds of behaviour or condemns others as intolerable to the living God. So far as the prophetic concern with conduct goes, we might almost say that the prophet is appointed by God to publish the statute law of Israel, to declare the will of the supreme Lawgiver to his subjects. In contrast to this the task of the king is to administer and enforce the statutes of God, and in so doing to produce a certain amount of what we should call 'case law'. The final codification in the *Torah*, with its 613 'Thou shalts' and 'Thou shalt nots', is in large measure the result of many generations of prophetic teaching and of governmental and judicial activity. And, be it noted, the final product is not in the form of a discussion of the nature of the good or of the categorical imperative: it is rather a catalogue of concrete things that must be done or not done, because that is the will of God.

two

JUDAISM AND
THE LAW OF MOSES

ONE very important conclusion from the preceding discussion is that when we speak of the Kingdom of God we are not to think of it primarily as a political organization which can be brought into existence by despotic decree or democratic legislation. For the Hebrew mind it is above all a personal relation between a king and his subjects. The relation is marked on the one side by the complete regal competence of the king, and on the other by the complete trust and loyalty of his subjects. This being so on the human level when the ancient Hebrew used the concept of kingship to describe the relation between God and his people, he thought in terms of complete sufficiency on God's part and complete loyalty on man's. One aspect of God's sufficiency consists in his being the final authority on matters of right and wrong; and complete loyalty on man's part calls for total obedience to such direction as God gives. That direction is embodied in what the Hebrews call the *Torah*, a term which is regularly translated in the Greek Bible by the word *Nomos* and in the English versions by the word 'Law'. 'Law' is in many ways a misleading translation because the fundamental idea of the Hebrew word *Torah*, and of the root from which it is derived, is not the idea that in our minds is associated primarily with law. We think of it in the first instance as

something that has been put on the statute book by enact-
ment of some competent authority, and the chief thing
about it is that it imposes an obligation on the subject to
obey an obligation backed by sanctions; so that he incurs
penalties if he does not do what is commanded and refrain
from what is forbidden. The idea that underlies the word
Torah is not primarily the formulation of a series of categorical commands and prohibitions with appropriate sanctions, though such an idea is part of its meaning. It is
rather a body of instruction regarding man's place in God's
world and his duties to God and his neighbour. The *Torah*
is the divine guidance as to the right way in which man
should behave as a subject of the heavenly king.

This great corpus of rules of conduct and concrete examples is traditionally ascribed as a whole to Moses. We
should rather regard it as the product of long development
over many centuries, with Moses having had a very large
part in setting the development in motion. This living,
growing body of rules, traditions, and examples becomes,
in the period after the Exile, the Rule of Life for Israel, the
formulation in plain terms of what might be called the
Israelite ideal. It becomes a fixed belief that the truly wise
man is the man who studies and comes to know intimately
this code of conduct, this completely reliable guide to the
art of living. That can be illustrated over and over again
from the Old Testament. Take for example these verses
from Psalm 19 (7–11):

*The law of the Lord is perfect, restoring the soul; the testimony
of the Lord is sure, making wise the simple. The precepts of the
Lord are right, rejoicing the heart; the commandment of the Lord is
pure, enlightening the eyes. The fear of the Lord is clean, enduring
for ever: the judgements of the Lord are true, and righteous*

*altogether. More to be desired are they than gold, yea, than much
fine gold: sweeter also than honey and the honeycomb. Moreover
by them is thy servant warned: in keeping of them there is great
reward.*

It is easy to see what is involved here; the study and practice of the *Torah* is for the devout Jew something more than
a religious exercise, something more than a way of behaving
well; it is a liberal education. By studying it you may not
only achieve virtue; you may also acquire the true wisdom.
The whole activity of the people whom the New Testament calls 'scribes' and Judaism 'Rabbis' is based on this
principle. By constantly turning this law of God over in
your mind and studying every detail of it you can become
a completely educated person. So the content of this code
comes to be looked upon as the very essence of wisdom.
There is nothing more worthy of man's attention and
study.

Similar sentiments are expressed by the author of that
amazing encomium of the *Torah*, Psalm 119. Verses 97 to
104 are a typical section:

*Oh how I love thy law! it is my meditation all the day. Thy
commandments make me wiser than mine enemies; for they are ever
with me. I have more understanding than all my teachers; for thy
testimonies are my meditation. I understand more than the aged,
because I have kept thy precepts. I have refrained my feet from
every evil way, that I might observe thy word. I have not turned
aside from thy judgements; for thou hast taught me. How sweet
are thy words unto my taste! yea, sweeter than honey to my mouth!
Through thy precepts I get understanding: therefore I hate every
false way. Thy word is a lamp unto my feet, and a light unto my
path!*

Just by concentrated attention to the *Torah* this man

claims that he is wiser than his enemies, and more understanding than his teachers and his seniors. He is no more
dependent on human guidance, for he has found the secret
of all wisdom and knowledge. Job 28 and Proverbs 8 and
9 tell a like story. No praise is too high for the *Torah*, and
in the end we find it identified with the wisdom of God
himself!

From the books of Proverbs, Ecclesiasticus[1] and the
Wisdom of Solomon we get the idea of wisdom as existing
before the creation of the world; and on the rabbinic side
this is matched by the idea that the Law existed before the
creation. The second century Rabbi Aqiba says 'The
instrument by which the world was created was the Law.'[2]
We may compare what is said in Proverbs 8.22–31. In the
pre-Christian era the word 'wisdom' has a variety of
senses. On the one hand it is the self-revelation of God, and
on the other it is the highest reach of man's knowledge. But

[1] Ecclesiasticus 15.1: 'He who fears the Lord', that is seeks wisdom,
'and he who takes hold of the Law will find her (wisdom)'.

Ecclesiasticus 34.8: 'The Law will be fulfilled where there is no false-
hood and wisdom will be the perfection of a trustworthy mouth.'

Ecclesiasticus 21.11: 'He who keeps the Law masters its meaning and
purpose, and wisdom is the crown of godly fear.'

Ecclesiasticus 19.20: 'All wisdom is fear of the Lord; and in all wisdom
there is the doing of the Law', that is to say three things, religion, wisdom
and obedience to the Law are aspects of the same achievement.

Ecclesiasticus 24.7–12. Here we have wisdom personified, speaking for
herself. Wisdom says 'With all these', that is all peoples and nations,
'I sought for a resting place and where I should lodge and in whose
inheritance I should find my lodging. Then the creator of all things gave
me a command, and he who created me set my bound and he said,
"Dwell thou in Jacob and take up thine inheritance in Israel". So I took
root among an honourable people in the portion of the Lord and of his
inheritance.'

[2] *Pirkē Aboth* 3.15 (see H. Danby, *The Mishnah*, p. 452).

that reach can only be achieved by accepting what is given by God, and it is at the same time the best possible achievement of man's effort.

We have now got to the point where we have a community, a nation whose governor is God. Its members have from God this clear idea as to where they will find their wisdom and their best life, and they are convinced that in following that revelation they can achieve true wisdom and a good life. Let us look a little further into the matter. We probably all realize that there is more to ethical conduct than just finding out what is the wisest thing to do, and then doing it successfully. We realize that underneath everything that is worth calling conduct in any serious sense of the word there lie springs of conduct—ideals, hopes, fears and so on—and that it is these that give character and quality to conduct. If the beggar calls at the back door it may or may not be that the right thing to do is to hand him half a crown or a packet of sandwiches. But if we only give them in order to get rid of him, that is a very different thing from giving because of sympathy for his hard lot. Nor must we suppose that that interest in the psychological background of behaviour is a completely new thing. The Jewish ethic is just as much aware of the motives of conduct as we are. It will clear up our ideas of ethics in Gospel times if we try to find out what were the springs of conduct for the devout and observant Jews.

The first clue is given by the daily religious obligations of every Jew, which is to recite morning and evening the passage known as the *Shĕma'*. The *Shĕma'* occupies in Judaism the place that is occupied in Christianity by the Apostles' Creed and the Lord's Prayer combined. If you can conceive an obligation on every devout Christian to say both

these morning and evening, that would be about equiva-
lent to the Jewish obligation to recite the *Shĕmaʿ*. It consists
of three passages of Scripture in this order: Deuteronomy
6.4–9, 11.13–21; Numbers 15.37–41. It is called *Shĕmaʿ*
because of the first word of Hebrew 'hear' ('Hear, O
Israel, the Lord our God is one Lord'). When the Jew per-
formed this daily ritual in his private prayers he 'took upon
himself the yoke of the kingdom'.[1] The 'yoke of the kingdom' at once called up a picture of two pairs of oxen doing
work for some Jewish farmer. When the devout Jew recited
this daily prayer he felt that he was harnessing himself to
God's plough, God's wagon, God's chariot, putting himself at God's disposal to do whatever God demanded him
to do. He did not go exploring on his own account: rather
he submitted his will to the will of the heavenly King and
went where he was commanded to go and did what he was
commanded to do. The technical name for the whole
system of obedience that is embodied in the Law is the
Hebrew word *hālăkhāh* which literally means 'walking'.
For the devout Jew the *hālăkhāh* is a royal road to walk in,
the King's highway, and it is laid down and marked out
and sign-posted. When the Jew in his public prayers in the
synagogue took part in the recitation of the *Shĕmaʿ* that was
regarded as the proclamation of the kingdom of God.
When you had the whole unit saying in unison the *Shĕmaʿ*,
each one speaking for himself, the kingdom of God was
proclaimed as a present fact. To proclaim the *Shĕmaʿ* was to
promulgate it as a royal decree.

Suppose there is a convert from paganism to Judaism,
what happens then? There is a fixed ritual for the reception
of proselytes, a ritual of initiation into a community whose

[1] See C. G. Montefiore and H. Loewe, *A Rabbinic Anthology*, p. 3.

life is to be lived in obedience to the will of God. At every stage it is impressed on the convert that this is the kind of life that he has to embrace. When he receives the prose-lyte's baptism he has selected commandments read to him, including not only what we should call the important ones dealing with the weighty matters of the Law, but also those that we might consider trivial or relatively unimportant, so that the stress is on the necessity of obedience to the revealed will of God in its wholeness and completeness. Both for the born Jew and the convert to Judaism it is a taking on one-self of the yoke of the Kingdom of God, and a proclama-tion of the kingdom in the life and worship of the com-munity. How is that worked out in detail? We may begin the answer in the light of a saying of the famous pre-Christian Jewish teacher, Simeon the Righteous, who declared that the world is based upon three things, that is to say a true and lasting civilization rests upon three foun-dations, the Law, worship, and 'the imparting of kind-nesses'.[1]

We have already said something about the Law. As it is presented here as a foundation of society it means the whole codified body of commandments giving the revealed will of God, a comprehensive system of rules covering the whole life of the Jew from the cradle to the grave, regulating his work and his worship, his family life and his relations with his neighbours. The development of it as a code extended over many centuries; and the form in which it was taken into the Old Testament canon was the form reached at the time that Palestine was part of the Persian Empire in the fifth century B.C. and the beginning of the fourth. What had been put together up to that time was attributed to Moses,

---

[1] *Pirkē Aboth* 1.2 (see H. Danby, *The Mishnah*, p. 446).

though in fact it was the result of contributions made by judges and kings, prophets and priests during a period of at least eight hundred years. It had two main characteristics. The first is an undivided loyalty to God. The Ten Commandments begin with an unqualified demand for this. It is important to remember the difference between Hebrew monotheism and the monotheism which we derive from Greek philosophical thought. The Greek comes to monotheism through the search for a single explanation for the variety of existence; what the Greek philosophers had been searching for from the beginning is a primary reality or first cause. The Hebrew comes to monotheism by a different road. He comes through the elimination of conflicting claims on loyalty and devotion. Hebrew monotheism is a worship that cannot and must not be shared. The second feature of Jewish Law is its full respect for human personality. There is, incidentally, a striking contrast in this respect between Hebrew law and Roman law. Hebrew law is much less concerned with the rights of property and much more concerned with the rights of personality. Hebrew and Jewish law, both the 'statute law' of the Pentateuch and the 'case law' of the scribal and rabbinical decisions, is primarily concerned with the rights of persons. This is brought out by Finkelstein in his book, *The Pharisees* (p. 66), in which he compares the Sadducees and the Pharisees. There were a number of legal issues on which they took different views, and a detailed examination of these goes to show that the rabbinical or Pharisaic view of the law and the application of it is almost always concerned to assert the rights and dignity of human beings without regard to their social status. They may be free or slave, it does not matter, but they have certain rights and dignities which must be preserved and safeguarded, and the interpretation of the Law is the way of seeking to do that.

Simeon's next foundation of civilization is worship. That means primarily the worship of the Temple, but in process of time it is expanded to cover the worship of the synagogue and the private worship of the individual. It is a highly significant fact that many of the rules concerning Jewish worship are embodied in the Law. That is contrary to the modern tendency in the West, which is to think that nothing of a religious nature is a matter of law. Acts of worship and acts of justice and mercy are alike part of the whole duty of man in Israel. By New Testament times the worship had developed far beyond what was prescribed in the Pentateuch. The rules there governed the Temple ritual; but many Jews seldom, if ever, took part in that ritual. Many never even saw the Temple; perhaps once in a lifetime they might get there for one of the major feasts, but as so many lived elsewhere the rules of the Pentateuch simply did not apply. A Jew living in Rome was under an obligation to present himself in Jerusalem three times a year. That was part of his religious duty. If he had tried to do it he would very likely have had to cease living in Rome altogether. Under such conditions a great many Jews could have kept the letter of the Law only by living in Palestine for six months of the year and going back home in the winter. Clearly this was not feasible, and Jews who were in this position obviously did not derive much good from the daily services in the Temple. They tried to find their normal form of worship in their private devotions and in the services of the synagogue. These things were part of the good Israelite's duty, his duty to God. His prayers and praises, his study of God's word, all were thought of as an offering to God. We are too prone in these days to think of acts of worship in psychological terms. Our main interest is apt to be in their effects on the worshipper. Many people assume that if they are not consciously uplifted by going to church there is no reason why they should continue to go. The Jewish way of looking at the matter was much more concerned with whether or not these acts of worship would be acceptable to God. The punctual performance of religious duties, with due reverence and a turning of the mind and heart towards God, was an obligation and a privilege whether the worshipper felt like it beforehand or not, and whether he felt better for it afterwards or not. The question whether he wanted to go to the synagogue at a set time had nothing to do with the case. His business was to be there. The question whether he felt better afterwards was also irrelevant. It is quite easy, as we all know, for dutiful worship of this kind to degenerate into the mechanical performance of rites that have ceased to have any real meaning to the performer. I do not think that is a serious danger today. We are more exposed in these days to the peril, from which the Jew was set free, of ceasing to worship because we are never in the mood, or because our half-hearted attempts produce no immediate and exciting emotional result.

The last of the three items in Simeon's list is the imparting of kindnesses. This is a phrase almost impossible to translate, yet it is of vital importance for our understanding of Jewish ethics. To say 'the imparting of kindnesses' hardly begins to bring out the wealth of meaning involved. *Hesed* is commonly translated by words like 'mercy' or 'loving kindness'. That brings us nearer to the root meaning, but it is not quite satisfactory because mercy is apt to be somewhat arbitrary. A good deal may depend on the mood at the moment of the person involved. I am much less likely to be merciful if I have a raging headache, when it is difficult to take a detached, much less a merciful, view. But the 'imparting of kindnesses' is not a matter of whims or liberality of decision, it is a settled way of maintaining personal relations; and it is always connected with the maintenance of relations between people who are in a covenant relation with one another. When we use the word 'covenant' the simplest way of understanding what is involved is by considering the relationship between husband and wife, parents and children, friend and friend, or members of the same society who have their association governed by common interests and common obligations. One can act according to the strict letter of the law in such relationships. In that case there is no 'imparting of kindnesses'; there is only justice. 'Imparting of kindnesses' comes in when we start doing more than is required by the strict letter of the law. Strict justice may require that I give three-quarters of my salary or wages to my wife for housekeeping; that is an obligation. But then there is the extra packet of cigarettes or the occasional brooch; that is where 'the imparting of kindnesses' comes in. When some member of a covenant group has not played the game, 'imparting of kindnesses' really means saying, 'So-and-so has behaved in such a way as to forfeit all his rights, but we will not let him lose them. His rights are going to be preserved in spite of the fact that he has forfeited them.' In human society this loyalty to the covenant relation and all that it involves expresses itself in acts of kindness and helpfulness which are the outward and visible expression of an inward and spiritual unity. The 'imparting of kindnesses' is the active kindness, comfort, and support, given by members of the covenant-people to one another, and springing from a deep sense that they are members one of another. It is something that cannot be legislated for, because its very nature is to be the spontaneous and gracious response of brotherly love to a brother's need. In practice, of course, it can be both a very exalting thing and a very degrading thing. We can practise it until it merely means 'you scratch my back and I'll scratch yours'. We can also lift it up to a level of spontaneous feeling of unity.

There are, then, these three foundations of any true and lasting civilization: the standard of conduct, the worship, and a brotherly feeling for one another. If any one foundation is missing the whole structure will suffer. There is an increasing number of people today who think that the defect of our civilization is the lack of the second of the three. We have rules and regulations in plenty. We have a number of striking instances of corporate solidarity. It is the lack of worship that poisons the other two. Let us take a further look into the way of achieving the good life, as it appeared to the Jews, and consider what should be the motives of action in the three areas of life which Simeon stresses. What is required in the attitude and spirit of the doer in order that his fulfilment of the Law, or his act of worship, or his brotherly kindness may be genuine? The Jewish answer to that is again in two technical terms.

Kawwānāh has to do with the inward attitude of the doer towards his actions. A rabbi said, 'It does not matter whether you achieve much or little: it does not matter whether you have a big job or a little job, the thing that matters is whether your heart is directed to heaven, whether your mind is directed to God.'[1] The nature of the occupation does not count. It does not matter whether the man in question is a rabbi or a farm labourer: it is all one. What does matter supremely is whether or not in doing the work his intention is to serve and obey God. *Kawwānāh* characteristically belongs to 'religion', in the technical sense, and to ethics as well. In religion, it is the concentration of the mind and heart in acts of worship so that they are a real offering of the self and not just a mechanical performance of the rite. In ethics, it is the intention to do the good act or abstain from the evil deed in conscious and willing obedience to the will of God. Rabbi Me'ir said 'Everything depends on the *Kawwānāh* of the heart.'[2] 'He who prays must direct his heart towards God'[3] (remembering 'heart' in Old Testa/ ment and rabbinic usage is regularly used when we should say 'mind'). Another rabbi, Raba, said, 'For *doing* a com/ mandment *Kawwānāh* is *not* required; for committing a sin *Kawwānāh is* required'.[4] That is, the good intention and the good deed have each a value. Man has credit with God for doing the good act. He has credit for intending the good act even if circumstances prevent him from carrying out his intention; but best of all if he has the good intention and carries it out. On the other hand, the intention to do wrong is the thing that makes the wrong act really bad; the act may be done in error or unintentionally without serious stigma. Rabbi Nehemiah said, 'If a man purpose to com/ mit a sin, God does not reckon it to him till he has done it, but if he purpose to fulfil a command, then although he has had no opportunity to do it, God writes it down to him

[1] Montefiore and Loewe, *A Rabbinic Anthology*, p. 272.
[2] *Op. cit.*, p. 272.
[3] *Op. cit.*, p. 274.   [4] *Op. cit.*, p. 275.

at once as if he had done it.'[1] It all comes to this, 'to the rabbis the love of God becomes both the supreme command of the Law and the supreme motive'.[2] This direction of the heart towards God simply means that the final governing motive of all ethical action must be a desire to please God, and that means that the spring of action becomes in the last resort the love of God, so that the command and the motive run into one another.

The other important technical term is what is called *Lishmāh*.[3] Taken literally it means 'for its name'. We can best translate it by saying 'for its own sake'. You do the thing that is right simply because it is right 'for its own sake' and have no ulterior motive whatever. Here again are a few rabbinic examples. Rabbi Banna'ah used to say, 'If one studies the Law for its own sake it becomes to him an elixir of life; but if one studies the Law not for its own sake, it becomes to him a deadly poison.'[4] 'He who busies him⁄self with the Law for its own sake causes peace in the upper and the lower family (i.e. among the angelic hosts and among the sages); he is as if he had built the upper and the lower palace; he protects the whole world; he brings near the redemption.'[5] 'For God's sake, out of love, and *lishmāh*, are really all equal to one another.'[6] 'Do the words of the Law for the doing's sake, and speak of them for their own sake. Make them not a crown with which to exalt thyself, or a hoe with which to weed.'[7] In other words, do not use the study of the Law either to foster your own pride, or to increase your own profits. 'God said to Moses, "Go

---

[1] *Op. cit.*, p. 275. [2] *Op. cit.*, p. 276.
[3] See G. F. Moore, *Judaism*, vol. II, pp. 96 ff.
[4] *A Rabbinic Anthology*, p. 277.
[5] *Op. cit.*, p. 277. [6] *Op. cit.*, p. 278. [7] *Op. cit.*, p. 278.

and tell the Israelites, 'My children, as I am pure, so be you pure; as I am holy, so be you holy, as it is said "Holy shall ye be, for I, the Lord your God, am holy".'¹ 'All man's good deeds must be done in conscious relation to God, and with the thought of love of him continually in his mind. To him alone is the glory, and he must ever be praised.'² And finally the statement often repeated and very impor-tant, 'All is in the hand of heaven except the fear of heaven.'³ That is to say, everything is in the power of God except to compel man's reverence. God can do everything except compel someone to worship him. The two con-cepts, *Kawwānāh* and *lishmāh*, both lie behind that saying.

I do not think that there can be any doubt that, for the rabbis, to do something for the sake of God is more funda-mental than to do it for its own sake. This appears from the frequency with which the doing of the will of God is stressed as the motive of conduct. The idea that a good deed should be done for its own sake is present; but it takes second place to the idea of obedience to God. Thus it is not allowed to ask why commandments dealing with what look like minor matters are given the same unqualified status as those dealing with highly important duties. It is pointed out that the same reward is attached to the 'major' com-mandment to honour father and mother as is attached to a 'minor' commandment. This is to show that it is not per-missible to discriminate in this way. Again, you must not ask why a garment of mixed stuffs is forbidden. It is enough that this is the will of your Father in heaven. Your business is to be swift and strong and courageous in obeying it, just because it is his will, and because to conform your will to God's is the only way to a secure and satisfying life.

¹ *Op. cit.*, p. 280. ² *Op. cit.*, p. 281. ³ *Op. cit.*, p. 291.

42

three

JESUS AND
THE LAW OF MOSES

WE have considered some of the principal ingredients in Jewish ethics in New Testament times, and it is clear that we are unjust if we represent Judaism as being indifferent to the motives for action. The contrary is the case: while the Jewish Law lays great stress on the punctual and meticulous performance of the duties published in the Law, it also lays stress on the necessity of doing the command for the right reasons. We saw that the two principal motives to which special value is attached are the doing of God's commandments just because they are his commandments and with a view to pleasing him, and doing a good deed for its own sake without any regard to what profit it is going to bring you. The one they called *kawwānāh* and the other *lishmāh*. The two are not inconsistent with one another. It is quite possible to do something with the idea of pleasing God and at the same time to do it for its own sake.

Up till now we have been looking at the ethic of the Old Testament as developed in the experience of the Hebrew people through the impact of divine revelation on the facts of life and history. It is important to remember that the ethical system set out in the Old Testament, and developed in the *Mishnāh* and *Talmûd*, is not an ethical system produced by philosophers thinking in the abstract. It is worked

43

out in the direct experience of life, by the impact of revelation on the hard facts of life and history; and they were hard
facts. Life in Palestine for the Chosen People was an affair
of almost constant turmoil and recurrent crises. There were
only two brief periods in the whole history of the Hebrew
occupation of Palestine when it could be said that the
people enjoyed relative peace, prosperity and security. These
periods, both short ones, covered the greater part of the
reigns of David and Solomon and the decades when the
Maccabean dynasty was in charge in the second and first
centuries B.C. The rest of the time life in their not very
fruitful land was under constant threat from neighbouring
great powers. Century after century the great Empires swept
backwards and forwards in a struggle for mastery of the
Fertile Crescent, and out of that constant crisis the Hebrew
people produced two things: a creed and a code; Jewish
monotheism and the Jewish Law. We have tried to look at
the creed and the code as they were seen by the contemporaries of Jesus, the first-century Jews. Now we must
take the next step and try to see them as they were seen by
him.

Is it necessary or desirable to do this? Would it not be
simpler to leave aside the Old Testament and Jewish background and start straight away on the New Testament?
That is something that the Christian Church from the
second century onwards has constantly refused to do, and
for very good reasons. Early in the second century of the
Christian era there was a very devout and saintly heretic
called Marcion who did his best to persuade the Church
to cut completely loose from this Jewish tradition. It was
his view that true Christianity had no roots in the Jewish
past. It was a completely new beginning. Christ had no

Jewish parentage: he appeared without warning, miracu-
lously, mature and full-grown in the synagogue at Caper-
naum on the Sabbath of which Luke tells us in chapter 4
of his Gospel, to reveal a God who had nothing in common with the God of the Old Testament. Marcion did not
deny that the Old Testament was true or that the God of
the Old Testament was a real God. What he did deny was
that the God of the Old Testament had anything to do
with the God and Father of Jesus Christ. They were two
quite different people. But the Church of the second century would have nothing to do with this theory. It held, as
the Church has held ever since, that the entire heritage into
which we have entered is precious. Jesus comes not to
destroy the Law and the Prophets but to fulfil them. He
fulfils them first by understanding them in their deepest
meaning, and second by going beyond them in action.

We must now try to follow Jesus' understanding of the
Jewish Law as it existed in his day. For that purpose we
can hardly find a better focusing point for our study than the
Sermon on the Mount, for it covers a great deal of the
ground in which we are interested. Before discussing its
details I must refer to the background of the Sermon as it is
understood as a result of what may be called the commonly
accepted critical studies of the Gospel of Matthew. We
have there a book made up by adding to the framework
supplied by Mark materials drawn from two other sources,
the source Q (from which Luke also borrowed) and the
source which for convenience is called M, covering the
material that is peculiar to Matthew. That is the usual
critical view. I should add a further element: the religious
and literary gift of St Matthew himself, whoever he was.
That literary and religious gift is often overlooked. It is

what St Paul calls a *charisma*, and I use the word advisedly in connexion with Matthew's editorial activities. We must not think of the evangelists as literary hacks producing gospels by stringing other people's work together; they were genuine composers, with gifts as authentic as those of the poet or the musician or the artist, and a good deal more important.

We must also realize that the five great discourses in Matthew, of which the Sermon on the Mount is the first, are not shorthand records of actual addresses delivered by the Prophet of Nazareth on specified dates at specified places. They are systematic presentations of the mind of Christ on various matters of great moment to his Church. The modern critical position is stated clearly enough by Dibelius in his book, *The Sermon on the Mount* (p. 105), in four propositions:

(1) The Sermon is made up by combining single sayings, which Jesus uttered on various occasions to different people.

(2) These sayings, combined by St Matthew or his source, no longer proclaim a heavenly kingdom, but describe a Christian life on earth.

(3) This involved some adaptation of particular sayings.

(4) The Sermon on the Mount is not the only programme of Christian conduct in the New Testament; but it overshadows all others as the great proclamation of the new righteousness.

I have a few comments to make on each of these four propositions.

(1) The statement that the Sermon is made up by combining 'single sayings'. That is true up to a point. But there is ample evidence in the Sermon itself that some of the

46

material that is given in it was more than 'single sayings', and that sayings were already combined into short pieces of teaching. For example we have in chapter 5 a number of passages which have a common form: 'You have heard that it was said to them of old time . . . but I say unto you . . .' It is quite clear that we have there a systematic treatment of a number of commandments in the Jewish Law, and I do not think it is in the least likely that this systematic treatment began life as a collection of oddments. It is much more likely that it comes from Jesus himself, and that he dealt with these half-dozen or so commandments at once and not merely in a series of separate sayings. The same holds for chapter 6, where we have a collection of three sayings about various kinds of religious observances.

(2) I think that Dibelius' second point is true. We have a good deal of evidence outside the Sermon on the Mount that parables and sayings, which originally were warnings to the man in the street to flee from the wrath to come, have been adapted by the early Church and have become pieces of good advice for those within the Christian community. One of the simplest and most striking is the piece of advice about coming to an agreement with your adversary in a lawsuit while still on the way to court, in case he takes you and hands you over to the judge, and the judge to the jailor, and you find yourself in prison until the last penny is paid! (Matthew 5.25 f.; Luke 12.57 ff.). It is probable that the original moral of that story was that men and women are living on the edge of judgment, that any moment now they may be called upon to render an account, that it is God with whom they will have to reckon, and that if they have not made their peace with God by repentance here and now they will be liable to find themselves in serious

trouble. The parable says in effect, 'If you are engaged in a lawsuit you have got enough sense to know it is better to settle it outside the court if you can. You have all got a law-suit with the Almighty and the day is coming when out-of-court settlement will no longer be open to you. Be warned!' But as we have it in the Gospels it has become a piece of good advice to Christian people in their everyday relation-ships. There are a number of other cases where a similar process can be discerned.

It is important to note that the contrast between the heavenly kingdom and life on earth can easily be pushed too far. In the first century men and women lived in a 'three-storey universe'; heaven above, earth on the ground floor, and the abode of shadows underneath. That of course is out of date scientifically. The important point about it for our purposes is that it was taken for granted by those who believed in it that the universe was one single establish-ment; it was not a three-storey establishment. Therefore an effective kingdom of God was not one which was only effective on the top storey and had no application anywhere else. It had to be effective on all three floors; and the belief that this is indeed the case runs through the New Testa-ment. The Lord's Prayer says: 'Thy will be done on earth as in heaven.' Jesus also said: 'If I by the finger of God cast out demons, then the kingdom of God has come upon you' (Luke 11.20). It is not possible to make a complete distinction between a heavenly kingdom and life on earth. What we may observe is a certain shifting of emphasis, and I think that Dibelius is right in pointing out that the main emphasis has shifted from the future consummation to the present realization. But I should hold that both elements are part of the authentic teaching of Jesus.

(3) It is true that the teaching involves some adaptation of particular sayings, but the amount can easily be exaggerated.

(4) On the point that there are 'other programmes of conduct in the New Testament than the Sermon on the Mount', that is also true, but it has to be understood in the light of considerations that I shall bring forward later.[1]

We have seen that the sources for the Sermon on the Mount from which the Evangelist has drawn his material are the document Q and his own private treasury, which has been called M. A great deal of the material used in the Sermon on the Mount was published in written form, and I should think in Aramaic, round about AD 50, and probably on the early side of 50. The other material, which is peculiar to Matthew, we cannot say very much about: it may or may not have been in documentary form before Matthew got it. All we can say is that it provides a group of teachings that have a strong family likeness.[2]

[1] See Chapter 4.

[2] Abbot B. C. Butler, *The Originality of Matthew*, gives priority to Matthew and regards the document Q as an unnecessary hypothesis. I do not think that this case will stand up to close criticism. We have to look at the material in Matthew's Sermon and compare it with the corresponding sections in Luke. Critical orthodoxy says that the pieces that we find in Luke are part of the raw or partly cooked material out of which St Matthew made the Sermon. Butler says that the Sermon is the source of the scattered fragments in Luke. That seems to me very fanciful. What we are asked to believe is that St Luke, who was himself a very considerable literary artist, found this noble discourse and could think of nothing better to do with it than hack it to pieces. Having done so he planted the battered torso in his own Gospel as the 'Sermon on the Plain', scattered some of the bits and pieces in other more or less unsuitable contexts, and discarded the rest. The motives suggested by Butler for the committing of these atrocities by St Luke (pp. 37–48) seem to me to be quite inadequate; and I find it more rational to suppose that St Matthew created the Sermon than that St Luke deliberately destroyed it.

If the Sermon on the Mount is genuine composition (and I say 'composition' and not 'compilation' or 'fabrication'; 'compilation' was the idea of the older literary criticism; 'fabrication' is what more recent and more radical criticism amounts to, even if it is not said outright; I say 'composition' and I use the word as I should use it of a classical symphony), then careful analysis of the argument is the first step towards understanding it. It is bad procedure to *begin* by trying to break it up into authentic sayings of Jesus, adapted sayings of Jesus, editorial glosses, and the like. That kind of work can only be done at the end of the enquiry. The first task is to understand what the Sermon as a whole and as it stands is trying to say. The task has often been attempted. The most fruitful analysis up to date is that of Windisch.[1]

We begin with a short narrative setting of the scene (5.1 f.). These two verses make a number of important points. They represent the Sermon not as broadcast propaganda, but as formal instruction given to a group of disciples assembled at a suitable quiet place to receive it, the hill-country of Galilee, which was less thickly populated than the plains. At the very outset we are warned against indulging in one of the most insidious and mischievous forms of wishful-thinking, that which says 'If only the principles of the Sermon on the Mount were accepted and applied by politicians, statesmen and industrialists how happy the world would be!' The Sermon is addressed to disciples, not to mankind in general. It does not deal directly with the affairs of the world at large. And in any case it is hardly to be expected that it should find a ready

[1] H. Windisch, *Der Sinn der Bergpredigt*; ET: *The Meaning of the Sermon on the Mount* (Westminster Press, Philadelphia).

market among men of the world, many of whom find even the ten commandments intolerably irksome. The Sermon is not saying: 'This is how men in general should live if they really want to build the kingdom of God on earth.' It is saying: 'This is how you who are in the kingdom of God must live if your citizenship is to be a reality.'

That brings us to the Introduction. The Sermon is addressed to disciples and it begins with Hearty Congratulations, commonly known as Beatitudes (5.3–12). Note that beatitudes and woes are not the same things as blessings and curses. Jesus never cursed the scribes and Pharisees: he uttered woes about them. It is one thing to utter woes and another to utter curses. What he said about scribes and Pharisees was that they were more to be pitied than laughed at. It is one thing to say that X is in danger of damnation and another to say 'X be damned'. Neither are beatitudes identical with blessings. They are congratulations to people on their present position, 'Yours is the kingdom of Heaven'; and on their future prospects, 'You will inherit the earth', 'You will be comforted and satisfied'. These blessings really mean how fortunate are those concerned, how lucky the poor in spirit, for the kingdom of Heaven is theirs; how lucky the meek for they shall inherit the earth. The fact is that these people are actually enjoying or about to enjoy great privileges. However there are no privileges without responsibilities, and so in 5.13–16 we have a statement of these responsibilities. The disciples have to be the salt of the earth and the light of the world. Where much is received, much is required. That is the order in which things happen in the Sermon. First the congratulations, the status, the promise; and only after that the charge, the responsibilities, the tasks. The gift of new life can only be appropriated and enjoyed by living the new life. It is the nature and quality of this new life that is now to be described in detail.

The description is divided into three main sections. I suggest that this threefold division is based upon an ancient and familiar maxim preserved in what was, and is, probably the most popular part of the rabbinic literature, the *Pirkē Aboth*, the Sayings of the Fathers.[1] There we are told the teaching of Simeon the Righteous, to which I have already referred, that the world rests upon three pillars: the Law, the worship and the 'imparting of kindnesses'.[2] The *Torah* is the law of the kingdom of God, that is to say God's revealed will as the standard and pattern of human conduct; the worship is the divinely ordained means of access to God's presence, the way of fellowship with him, and the 'imparting of kindnesses' is the practical expression of brotherhood and corporate solidarity within Israel, a mutual loyalty within the covenant, shown in thought, word and deed.

The Sermon takes these fundamentals of Judaism and restates them as fundamentals of the New Israel living under the New Covenant. So we have the New Law (5.17–48), the New Standard of Worship (6.1–34), and the New Standard of Corporate Solidarity (7.1–12). The account of the New Law has a clearly marked beginning and end. It begins in verse 17 with the statement 'Do not imagine that I have come to destroy the law or the prophets: I have not come to destroy but to fulfil. For I tell you that until heaven and earth pass away, one jot or one tittle shall in no wise pass away from the law, till all be fulfilled.

---

[1] See H. Danby, *The Mishnah*, pp. 446–460.
[2] *Pirkē Aboth* 1.2 (Danby, p. 446).

Whoever therefore shall relax one of the least of the commandments, and teach other men to do so, shall be called least in the kingdom of heaven: but whoever does and teaches them he shall be called great in the kingdom of heaven. But I tell you that unless your righteousness exceeds the righteousness of the scribes and Pharisees you shall by no means enter the kingdom of Heaven.' There it begins, and it goes steadily on to verse 48 where the matter is summed up in a single statement: 'You therefore must be perfect, as your heavenly Father is perfect.' That means that the ultimate standard is God the Father himself. But when we turn to the actual content of the Law as set out, we find that knowledge of the Father is through the Son: there is real concrete instruction given in the form '*I* tell you'. This 'I tell you' is something that is presented to the followers of Jesus both in word and deed. It is very difficult to find anything in the way of positive instruction in the Sermon on the Mount that cannot be paralleled in the actual conduct of the Preacher of the Sermon. Whatever else may be true of the Sermon on the Mount, it is not a sermon that says 'Do as I say and not as I do'. This is borne out by the introduction of the New Law, particularly in 5.17 f., and especially in the words 'I have not come to destroy but to fulfil'. It is to be noted that these words are said not of prophecy alone, but of the Law and the Prophets. 'Do not suppose that I come to fulfil *either* the Law *or* the Prophets. I come to fulfil both now.' That means, in the broadest sense, that what has to be fulfilled is the terms of the covenant, including both the commandments and promises of God. The commandments are in the Law and, roughly speaking, the promises in the Prophets. These two things together make up the terms of the covenant between

God and his people. You fulfil a prophecy by making it come true: you fulfil a command by obeying it. To fulfil the Law and the Prophets is thus to make the New Covenant a reality, a reality into which men may enter forthwith. When they do, they become subject to its New Law; and the New Law is the holy will of God made visible in the obedience of Christ.

Turning to the contents of the New Law we observe that the framework is in the form 'You have heard that it was said to them of old time . . . but I say to you'. That formula occurs five times, introducing pronouncements on such things as murder, adultery, perjury, punishment, and communal loyalty. The tendency in the past has been to make the difference between Jesus and those who went before him something like this: that the old Law simply insisted on the outward good, whereas Jesus insists on the inward motive. This will not do. We have already seen that the Jewish ethic *did* insist on inward motive as well as on outward good. The difference lies elsewhere, and we will come to it in due course.

I turn now to the second important section, dealing with the new Worship (6.1–34). Here again we have a recurrent formal structure. There is the general introduction: 'Beware that you do not your righteousness before men, to be seen of them; else you have no reward with your Father which is in heaven. When you are doing charity do not sound a trumpet before you, as the hypocrites do in the synagogues and in the streets, that they may have glory of men. Verily I say unto you, they have received their reward. And when you are praying do not be like the hypocrites: for they love to stand and pray in the synagogues and in the corners of the streets, that they may be seen of men. Verily I say unto you, they have received their reward.' In verse 16 we come to the third section which has to do with fasting. 'When you fast do not be like the hypocrites, of a sad countenance: for they disfigure their faces, that they may be seen of men to fast. Verily I say unto you, they have received their reward. But when you fast, anoint your head, and wash your face; that you be not seen of men to fast, but of your Father which is in secret: and your Father, which seeth in secret, shall reward you.'

In these three instances we have the fixed form in which the teaching is presented. It is interesting to pause for a moment on the three things that make up the content of worship as understood in the Sermon. Prayer and fasting are not entirely surprising, but why almsgiving as a parti-cularly religious exercise? It is significant that after the destruction of the Temple in A.D. 70 and the consequent cessation of the sacrificial ritual, it was laid down by the rabbis, who set to work to pick up the pieces of Judaism, that almsgiving would be in God's eyes an acceptable sub-stitute for sacrifice. It is therefore perhaps not surprising that the section on the new Worship has a lot to say about alms-giving. Matthew 6.2-4 prescribes secret almsgiving as parallel to secret prayer and fasting. Another passage fur-ther on (6.19–21) deals with treasure in heaven; and we learn from other sources how treasure in heaven is acquired (Mark 10.21). Then there is the further saying about the good and evil eye (6.22 f.). In this context it is more than likely that the good eye signifies generosity and the evil eye meanness. Finally there is the statement in verse 24 that the kind of service that the new worship calls for cannot be divided between two masters, 'You cannot serve God and Mammon'. As a corollary to this, freedom from care and anxiety is inculcated in 6.25–34. Almsgiving, prayer and fasting alike point this way. The simple trust in God which is involved in true prayer, the generosity of true almsgiving, the self-denial of true fasting, all involve a certain sitting loose to possessions and a consequent release from anxiety.

In chapter 7 we have a statement of the need for right relations with our neighbours, the demand for a new spirit of corporate solidarity. It opens, interestingly enough, with a prohibition of censoriousness. One of the standing dangers of moral achievement under any ethical system is that we begin 'to trust in ourselves that we are righteous and despise others' (Luke 18.9). That is one of the things that cannot be tolerated in the New Israel. And it is very significant that the first duty towards one's neighbour is the duty of not looking down one's nose at him. At the same time there must be some discrimination, 'Do not give the holy thing to the dogs and do not cast pearls before swine.' What is in mind is that there must be, in the nature of things, some reserve; there is a duty to maintain and safeguard good and holy things, as well as a duty to be kind to others. Christians are required to follow the 'friend of publicans and sinners' (Luke 7.34), but they have also to keep constantly in mind that the level of the association was fixed by him and not by them: they met on his ground and not on theirs. This section ends with a general statement of the covenant rule for relations with our neighbours. That is expressed in the Golden Rule; things that you would like people to do to you, you should similarly do to them, for this is 'the Law and the Prophets', or as we might put it, this is the essence of the covenant.

In 7.13–29 we have the summing up of the whole matter. First in verses 13–14 it is emphasized that there is a choice to be made and a decision taken; in verses 15–20 there are warnings against people who would divert attention from the real issues; in verses 21–23 there is a clear statement of the necessity for real decision as distinct from mere verbal profession; this is followed in verses 24–27 by the parable of two believers. In verse 28 the evangelist ends with his regular formula 'And it came to pass that when Jesus had finished these sayings, the multitudes were astonished at his teaching: for he taught them as one having authority, and not as their scribes'.

When we look at the Sermon as a whole, we have to ask whether it gives a fair picture of Jesus's attitude to, and his understanding of, the Jewish spiritual heritage. I think that in the main it does. There is a great deal in it that can be paralleled from Jewish sources. That was brought out in a rather polemical way by a well-known Jewish rabbi, Gerald Friedlander, in his *Jewish Sources of the Sermon on the Mount*. His main thesis was that any good in the Sermon on the Mount can be paralleled from Jewish sources, and that nothing that cannot be paralleled from Jewish sources is any good. That is a distorted and polemical way of saying that the Sermon on the Mount takes the best and deepest things in the Jewish creed and code of conduct and adds to them the still deeper insights of Jesus himself. If we ask what these deeper insights are, the answer must be they are the things embodied in his Messianic Ministry. And it is to that we must now turn.

four

THE FOUNDATION OF CHRISTIAN
ETHICS: FOLLOWING CHRIST

I HAVE suggested that Jesus summed up the New Law in the commandment: 'Be ye perfect as your heavenly Father is perfect.' This does not mean setting up some completely new and unheard of ethical standard to replace the existing standard of the Old Testament and of Judaism. On the contrary the very form of the new commandment immediately reminds us of the old commandment of the Law: 'Ye shall be holy, for I the Lord your God am holy' (Leviticus 19.2). The Jewish rabbis had fastened on that commandment and construed it in their own way as calling upon God's people to be separated from all the abomina‑ tions of the surrounding heathenism. The required holiness was to be modelled on the white‑hot purity of God in whose presence evil cannot survive. Jesus does not deny that ideal. He adds to it. He asks not merely that his fol‑ lowers should keep clear of the contagion of evil; but also that they should show in their lives some positive quality akin to the positive creative goodness of God.

'Be ye perfect as God is perfect.' That is a very tall order. It is worth our while to pause for a moment on this motion of 'perfection'. A good way of approaching it is by con‑ sidering what is meant by the doctrine of the 'sinlessness' of Jesus. Obviously this cannot be historically demonstrated: we know only a small fraction of the total thoughts, words, and deeds of Jesus. Anything we say must be based on these samples. If we predicate that Jesus was perfect as his Father in heaven is perfect, it must be in virtue of some discernible quality in the samples of his conduct that we possess.

Here it becomes relevant to consider 'perfection' as we use the term in relation to a work of art. For every artist there comes a moment when he has to say, 'This is as good as I can make it. Any change after this will be for the worse.' Not only can he not better it. Neither can we. The art in question may 'progress' in all kinds of ways; but not even Beethoven attempts to revise Bach or Mozart. But a Brahms can write variations on a theme of Haydn. Is there not about the words and deeds that make up the ministry of Jesus a moral quality analogous to the artistic quality that makes a great masterpiece of music or poetry or painting? And is not the challenge of 'Be ye perfect . . .' a challenge to produce words and deeds of a quality similar to that which we discern in those of the Master, and to follow him (Matthew 19.21)?

Is there any brief and compendious way in which we can describe what is involved in following Christ? One thing can be said right away. To follow Christ is not to go in pursuit of an ideal but to share in the results of an achievement. Christ does not ask anyone to go where he has not already been himself, or to do anything that he has not already done himself. The stiffest question he asks a disciple is, 'Can you drink the cup that I drink, and share in the baptism that I undergo?' (Mark 10.35–45; Matthew 20. 20–28). With him we are never on uncharted ways for he is always ahead of us. He sends no man to warfare at his own charges. Or in the words of Richard Baxter[1]

[1] Lines from his *Poetical Fragments* (1681) which appear in many hymn books in stanzas beginning 'Lord, it belongs not to my care'.

Christ leads me through no darker rooms
Than he went through before;
And he that to God's kingdom comes
Must enter by this door.

Now we can go a step further in the search for what is
involved in following Christ. The starting point is the
story told in St Mark (12.28–34):

One of the scribes, who had been listening to the
debate between Jesus and the Sadducees, and had ob-
served how well he answered them, came forward and
put the question, 'Which is the first commandment of
all?' Jesus replied, 'The first commandment is, "Hear O
Israel, the Lord our God, the Lord is one: and thou shalt
love the Lord thy God with all thy heart and all thy soul
and all thy understanding and all thy strength." And
here is the second, "Thou shalt love thy neighbour as
thyself." There is no other commandment greater than
these.' 'Well spoken, Master,' said the scribe; 'What you
say is quite true. For he is one, and there is no other
beside him; and to love him with one's whole heart and
understanding and strength, and to love one's neighbour
as oneself is a far bigger thing than all the burnt offerings
and sacrifices.' This reply showed Jesus that the man
was thinking seriously, and he said to him, 'You are not
far from the kingdom of God.' After that nobody ven-
tured to put any more questions to him.

It has often been suggested that here we have the quintessence of Christian ethics. The two great commandments
sum up the whole duty of a Christian man; and the great
originality of Jesus lies in the fact that out of the vast corpus

of Jewish Law and tradition he chose just these two precepts and gave them an absolute priority over all the others.
There is a measure of truth in this view; but it has to be
qualified in several points. Let us look at the incident a
little more closely. What is reported is a talk between two
Jews in Jerusalem in the early thirties of the first century.
One is a professional scholar, an expert in the interpretation
of the Law and the tradition. The other is the Galilean
teacher Jesus of Nazareth. They are discussing the Jewish
way of life, and the particular point in debate is whether it
is possible to find in the Law any single, simple, and all-
embracing rule of behaviour. Jesus says 'Yes: among all the
commandments, that found in Deuteronomy 6.4, "Hear
O Israel . . ." comes first' (it was part of the *Shěma'*, and
therefore part of the daily obligation of every devout Jew to
repeat in his prayers); 'and—for good measure—the second
is "Thou shalt love thy neighbour as thyself" (Leviticus
19.18). No other commandment takes precedence of these.
All others give place to them.' The parallel passage in St
Matthew (22.40) has the statement that the whole of the
Law and the Prophets depends on these two commandments.

All this, however, adds up to the somewhat unexpected
result that the two great commandments are presented by
Jesus and accepted by the scribe as the quintessence, not of
Christian ethics, but of the Jewish Law. It can further be
urged that closer examination of the second great commandment shows that it lacks something. I am to love my
neighbour as I love myself. How do I love myself? Most
of us, if we are candid, must answer 'selfishly'. To love my
neighbour as myself may therefore be no more than a kind
of sublimated selfishness. Be that as it may, there is no

escape from the fact that these two commandments are the quintessence of *Jewish* ethics.

What then is the differentia of Christian ethics? The answer to this question was clearly expressed a century ago by the famous English preacher F. W. Robertson of Brighton. It is in the sixteenth sermon of the series preached at Brighton.[1] The secret is the text in the Fourth Gospel (13.34): 'I am giving you a new commandment; it is that you love one another. As I have loved you, you are to love one another.' 'As I have loved you'; that is the character-istic and hall-mark of the gospel ethic. The injunction is repeated later on in these Farewell Discourses in St John's Gospel: 'This is my commandment, that you love one another as I have loved you' (15.12). We may note the occasion of these sayings. They belong to the night before the Crucifixion. The first promulgation of the *new* com-mandment comes in the discourse after the footwashing and can be linked up with an earlier statement concerning it, 'I have set you an example, that you should do as I have done to you' (John 13.15).

Why was Peter unwilling that Jesus should wash his feet? He wanted Jesus to love him, but he also wanted Jesus to keep his dignity. This utter self-giving shocked him: it seemed to him abject and almost grovelling. 'Lord thou shalt never wash my feet' means, 'You don't know what is due to yourself; I do, and I am not going to let you demean yourself in this way.' But Jesus insists on demeaning him-self in this way and doing for his friends what was slave's work.

[1] F. W. Robertson (1816–53). His sermons have been published in various editions since they were first issued posthumously in 1855, 1857 and 1863.

The second promulgation of the new commandment comes later the same evening. Its immediate context is the thought of the swiftly approaching Passion and the laying down of the Messiah's life for his friends. 'Love as I have loved you' calls for a love which has forgotten the meaning of self-regard, of what we call 'looking after number one'. It is totally unselfish. It is love of the quality that marks the Ministry of Jesus all through and reaches its crowning manifestation on the Cross. As St Paul puts it, 'He loved me and gave himself for me' (Galatians 2.20). This total self-giving is the characteristic feature of the ethic of Jesus. We may note four key points about it:

(1) It is not merely an ideal: it is act and deed. It is the way Jesus carries out his life-work.

(2) It goes beyond the highest requirement of the existing Hebrew-Jewish code by requiring a more complete love of neighbour than is involved in loving him as much as, or in the same way that, I love myself.

(3) In doing this it does not abrogate the old standards; for *love* is still the essential thing in the teaching of Jesus as it is in Leviticus and Deuteronomy. It does not abrogate: it fulfils. Jesus shows what is really involved in love of neighbour; and shows it in thought, word, and deed.

(4) As we have already seen it is not the case (as many think) that Jesus stressed the inward springs of action, the motives by which we are led, as against Judaism which was concerned merely with outward acts. Not only is such a view unjust to Judaism, which had a lot to say about *kawwānāh* and *lishmāh*, but it also fails to bring out the true significance of the teaching of Jesus. Hatred and lustful desire are not just unhealthy psychological conditions in the person who has them: they are wrongs done to the

person towards whom these thoughts are directed. What Jesus is saying is that if you are to love your neighbour with the kind of love that God requires you must not only treat him rightly and speak to him rightly; you must think about him rightly. To love as Christ loves means to put so high a valuation on your neighbour that it will be as impossible for you to harbour evil thoughts about him as to do him a physical injury.

It may be asked what harm hate in the heart or lust in the eye do to anyone but the person who harbours them. But it does not require much sensitiveness to the nuances of human behaviour to know that hate can be felt outside the hater without a word spoken or a hand raised; and there can be a horrible awareness of the predatory eye. In fact the modern emphasis on the inner springs and motives of action is appropriate to the formulation of the ethical ideal as one of self-realization rather than that taught and lived by Jesus. It is this ethic of self-realization which leads to the explicit or implied corollary that wrong-doing is most harmful to the wrong-doer. So we get in many quarters a general attitude that forgets the wrongs done to the victims of crime (always more than the wrongs of the individual actually robbed, raped, or murdered) in concern for the psychological health of the criminal and enthusiasm for reforming him. The Prodigal does not say 'I am the victim of a psychological upset'; he says, 'I have sinned *against heaven* (i.e. God) and in thy sight' (Luke 15.21). More concern about the wrong done would balance matters, and that means at least two things, that the wrong-doer must admit that he has done wrong, and that he must make reparation.

The new commandment given and lived by Jesus therefore goes beyond Jewish ethics, but does not abrogate it.

'I am not come to destroy the Law and the Prophets but to fulfil' (Matthew 5.17). We can see how profoundly true that is when we put three sayings together. *The Law* says: 'Ye shall be holy, for I the Lord your God am holy.' *The Sermon on the Mount* says: 'Be ye perfect as your heavenly Father is perfect.' *The Farewell Discourse* says: 'Love as I have loved you.' The ethical demands of the Law and the Prophets are not cancelled; they have become flesh and have dwelt among us in the person and work of our Lord Jesus Christ.

What then? Are we left with a new and still more exact-ing code than that of the Jewish law? Are we left with a supremely noble and heroic example which we are to try, however vainly, to follow? This is no good news! It also leaves two major problems on our hands. The first is that of seeing how the new standard is to be applied to the life of our own day. The second is that of finding the power to put into action what we see to be the right and good thing. These are in fact our urgent and practical problems, but the Christian way of approaching them frees them from the feeling of being an intolerable burden as they might at first appear to be.

We must recall the fact that the ethic of the Bible, from beginning to end is the ethic of the kingdom of God. In the Christian era that means that Christ is reigning in the world as God's vicegerent. He is *reigning*. In terms of Semitic kingship, that is of kingship as understood in the Bible, it means that we can look to him for reliable direc-tion on our moral problems, as Semitic peoples looked to their kings. The nature of Christ's kingship, however, is such that it has very different corollaries for the problems of Christian behaviour.

(1) We cannot fall back on mere legalism. The Sermon on the Mount, if made into a new cast-iron Law, will only produce a new Pharisaism, more intolerant and more intolerable than the old.

(2) We cannot be content with mere mechanical imitation of Christ. Progress in painting does not come by copying the old masters, though copying is an essential part of the artist's training. Jesus called the Twelve to be with him and learn his ways, and then to go out and do things for him. Each situation that calls for our action is unique and demands a unique response.

(3) We must bring to the task of Christian living a creative initiative, based on the Law and the Prophets, instructed by the words and deeds of Jesus, and able with him as guide to deal constructively and imaginatively with the problems of our time.

An illustration from the world of music will give an indication of what I mean. Sir Donald Tovey writes: 'Classical counterpoint is harmony stated in terms of a combination of melodies: classical harmony, when correctly translated from whatever instrumental conditions may have disguised it, is the result of good classical counterpoint where the minor melodic lines are not meant to attract attention. Modern counterpoint tends actually to avoid classical harmony. It prefers that simultaneous melodies should collide rather than combine; nor does it try to explain away the collisions. It wishes the simultaneous melodies to be heard; and if they harmonize classically the combination will not assert itself as such. Hence modern counterpoint is no longer a technical matter at all; its new hypothesis has annihilated it as a discipline. But this very fact has thrown new responsibilities on the composer's imagination. A technical discipline becomes a set of habits which, like civilization itself, saves the artist from treating each everyday matter as a new and separate fundamental problem. The rule-of-thumb contrapuntist need not trouble to imagine the sound of his combination; his rules and habits assure him that it cannot sound wrong. The composer who has discarded those rules and habits must use his imagination for every passage that he writes without their guidance. It is by no means true that mere haphazard will suit his purpose. Nor, on the other hand, is it true that any great classical master used rules as a substitute for his imagination. One of the first essentials of creative art is the habit of imagining the most familiar things as vividly as the most surprising. The most revolutionary art and the most conservative will, if they are both to live, have this in common, that the artist's imagination shall have penetrated every part of his work. To an experienced musician every score, primitive, classical, or futurist, will almost at a glance reveal the general question whether the composer can or cannot use his imagination.'[1]

Something like this has to happen in the ethical sphere.

We are living in the kingdom of God under the rule of Christ. Christ is adequate to all the demands that we can make on him. As with the good king in the Hebrew idea of kingship, we can rely on his judgment. This means that we are not tied hand and foot to a written code. Equally we are not left to our own devices. We have before us the records of the kingdom in the Old Testament, the New Testament, and Church History. From those records we can learn about the ways of the kingdom. But we have also

[1] *Essays in Musical Analysis*, vol. iii, pp. 220 f. Quoted by kind permission of the Oxford University Press.

a living king; and we have the assurance of his direct aid through his spirit as we seek to understand and apply the will of God in our own affairs. The springs of revelation are not dried up. The living Christ is there to lead the way for all who are prepared to follow him.

More than that, the strength to follow is there too. The living Christ still has two hands, one to point the way, and the other held out to help us along. So the Christian ideal lies before us, not as a remote and austere mountain peak, an ethical Everest which we must scale by our own skill and endurance; but as a road on which we may walk with Christ as guide and friend. And we are assured, as we set out on the journey, that he is with us always, 'even unto the end of the world' (Matthew 28.20).

five

THE EARLIEST
CHRISTIAN COMMUNITY

UP till now we have been surveying the ethical
ideals of the Old Testament and of early Judaism,
and we have tried to understand the way in which
Jesus fulfilled these ideals in the words and deeds of his
ministry. That ministry had a sequel. There came into
existence a new social organism, the Christian community,
the Church, the New Israel, the Body of Christ. In the
next chapter we shall see how this community held as one
of its most treasured possessions the *corpus* of teaching which
laid down the law of Christ and which showed ways in
which its principles could be applied to human affairs in
all their variety and complexity. But first we must consider
the Church itself as the *milieu*, the environment, of Christian ethics; the order of society in which the law of Christ
is the law.

It is important that we should avoid the anachronistic
reading back into the first century of later ideas and actual-
ities. It is through doing this that many people have come
to deny the authenticity of the sayings about the Church
attributed to Jesus in St Matthew 16.18 and 18.17. You
start off with the idea that Church means an ecclesiastical
organization with Archbishops, Bishops, Moderators,
Sung Eucharists, Prayer Meetings and the like: then you
realize that these things were probably not in existence in

the early decades of the Church and that Jesus cannot have had them in mind; then you conclude that he cannot have used the word 'church'. But this is simply because you have already put your own meaning on the word 'church' and have not stopped to ask what he meant by it, supposing he used it. As a matter of fact the word 'church' was in existence long before the time of churches—at least the word we translate by 'church'. The Hebrews had a word for it; the Greeks had a word for it; the Greek-speaking Jews had a word for it. The word put into the mouth of Jesus in Matthew is the word *ecclēsia*. It is quite a common word in the Septuagint (or Greek version of the Old Testament). It is regularly used to translate perfectly the Old Testament word *Kāhāl*. Now the *Kāhāl* was something that had been in existence for centuries before the beginning of the Christian era. The idea of the *Kāhāl* was already familiar to the Christians of Galilee, Judæa, Jerusalem and Damascus in the second quarter of the first century. But *ecclēsia* in Greek and *Kāhāl* in Hebrew did not mean the kind of church structure that we find in the third quarter of the second century where there is a well-organized community of bishops, presbyters, deacons and readers, organized primarily for what we should call religious exercises in the strict sense of the word.[1] It meets at regular intervals, under proper direction, to hold religious services, of which the most important is the eucharist. This is at the latter end of the second century; but it is not there in the first half of the first century.

We can go further than this. If it is wrong to think of the

---

[1] Cf. *The Apostolic Tradition* of Hippolytus (various editions) which contains details of rites and practices presumably in use at Rome in the early third century.

Christian community of the thirties and forties of the first century as much the same kind of institution as we find 150 to 200 years later, it is nearly as wrong to suppose that the Christian community immediately after the resurrection should be thought of as a synagogue of the Jewish pattern, or even as an eccentric kind of synagogue. The forms of worship in the Church borrowed a good deal from those of the synagogue. But, so far as I can see, all the evidence from the New Testament suggests that the members of the primitive Church in the thirties and forties thought of themselves neither as a synagogue, nor as a church in our way of thinking, that is primarily as a group for holding religious services. Historically the *Kāhāl* or the *ecclēsia* is not primarily a prayer meeting or religious gathering. It is the people of God, functioning as a people in the full exercise of all their communal activities and not just in their organized religious observances in some sacred edifice. I am very much inclined to think that we should look for the nearest analogy to the structure of government of the primitive Palestinian Christian community in those other communities of which we have begun to learn a great deal more in recent times. We have had for a long time a certain amount of information, limited in quantity but interesting in quality, regarding the community of the Essenes. We know about them from Josephus[1] and other authorities. We also know from Philo[2] about another community in Egypt called the Therapeutae. The discovery of a great horde of Jewish documents in the old synagogue near Cairo[3] at the end of last century brought to light another sect or group, that known under various names but most

[1] See *The Jewish War*, II. viii. 6.
[2] *de vita contemplativa* 2 (12).   [3] See P. Kahle, *The Cairo Geniza*.

frequently as the Covenanters of Damascus. The recent discoveries of the Dead Sea Scrolls have shed more light on that particular group, or if not on that group, on some other group very closely allied to it; but they look as if they were the same. The characteristic of all these groups, with the possible exception of the Therapeutae, is that they are not content simply to organize religious beliefs and worship; they are concerned with the whole range of the life of the society. In some ways they resemble monastic communities in that the members share a common life, which includes a great deal of religious observance, but also includes other things which we should not regard as directly religious work, meals, friendship, intercourse with one another, all governed by the rules of the community.

When we look at the early Church as it is described in Acts, we are apt to be a little blinded by the fact that it is so full of public addresses. Periodically St Peter gets up and preaches sermons to the general public: these sermons occur so regularly[1] that we tend to think of the life of the early Church as having consisted in meetings for public worship at which somebody preached a sermon. If we look a little more closely we get a different impression.

Let us begin with the question in the first chapter of Acts, where at verse 6 we are presented with a picture of the disciples talking with the Risen Lord after the resurrection and putting a question to him: 'Lord, are you restoring the kingdom to Israel at this present time?' He answered, 'It is not for you to know the times or the seasons, which the Father has set under his own authority. But this is what will happen: you will receive power when the Holy Spirit has come upon you, and you will be my

---

[1] Acts 1.15–22; 2.14–36; 3.12–26; 4.8–12.

72

witnesses both in Jerusalem, and in the whole of Judaea and Samaria and to the farthest limits of the country (or the earth).' That is the first intimation of what the original followers of Jesus were looking for after the resurrection, and of what they were instructed to expect. They were looking for the restoration of the kingdom of Israel, that is the restoration of national autonomy. At this point I refer you to Vernon Bartlett, the church historian, for an exposition of the bearing of this conversation on our ideas of the Catholic Church. He points out rightly that this question, by its national conception of the kingdom to be restored, was a purely Jewish view of the form of the kingdom. It was on a national and not on a universal basis: that is to say, it was not a Catholic Church at all.[1] What they are to expect is not the restoration of national autonomy, still less the establishment of an Israelite world empire. What they are to expect is the visitation of the Holy Spirit, which will bring to them power, and in that power they will be witnesses in Jerusalem, Judaea, Samaria and to the farthest frontier of the country, or the earth as the case may be (the word *gē* can mean either). It is interesting to notice that only Judaea and Samaria are mentioned: there is nothing about Galilee. It has been suggested by Lohmeyer that Galilee did not need to be mentioned because it was already well filled with Christians. It was already Christian territory.[2]

As the chapter continues we learn that after the departure of the Risen Lord the disciples returned to Jerusalem and went into the upper room. Then it says: 'All these were assiduous with one accord in prayer, along with the women

---

[1] V. Bartlett, *Church Life and Church Order*, pp. 26 ff.
[2] *Galiläa und Jerusalem*, p. 52.

and Mary the mother of Jesus and with his brethren. And at that time Peter stood up in the midst of the brethren and said (and the number of persons gathered together was about 120).' That is significant, for according to the *Mishnah* 120 is the minimum number of Jews to form a community and to have a Sanhedrin of their own.[1] Then we learn how they took steps to fill the vacancy caused by the death of Judas Iscariot. Now what is the purpose of that step? The first thing to be realized is that it is unique in the history of the Church: it is never done again. In Acts 12.2 we read that Herod Agrippa put James the son of Zebedee to death; but no attempt was made to fill that vacancy. Evidently, the place of James was not regarded as vacant, unlike the place of Judas. You cannot lose a place by death, you can only lose it by misconduct; Judas had lost his place not by the fact that he was dead, but by the fact that he was a traitor.

This way of looking at things can best be understood if we keep in mind that the early Church was thinking in terms of a speedy return of Christ to wind up the present order and to bring in a completely new order. One of the things that would happen at his coming was that the martyrs, the righteous dead, would be raised to receive their reward. The obvious reward of a man like James the son of Zebedee would be to receive what in fact was promised to the Twelve in the Gospels, where Jesus says 'I covenant to you as my Father has covenanted to me a kingdom, and you shall sit at table with me in my kingdom, and you will sit on thrones judging the twelve tribes of Israel' (Luke 22.29–30; cf. Matthew 19.28). That promise could not be nullified by the violent action of a secular ruler; it could

[1] See H. Danby, *The Mishnah*, p. 383.

74

only be violated by man's own misconduct. We must realize that it is the filling up of a vacant place on the ruling body of the New Israel that is in question. This post, to which Matthias was appointed in the place of Judas, is described by three different names: episcopate (Acts 1.20; AV 'bishopric'); superintendence (Acts 1.25; AV 'ministry'); apostolate (Acts 1.25). Episcopate makes us think of all the ideas which we now associate with bishops, but we must take the word in its plain meaning and not as an ecclesiastical technical term. The post is next called a diaconate, so we will have to make Matthias a deacon as well as a bishop. The deacon is minister or servant. And in the third place the post is called an apostolate, which means that Matthias would be similar to the apostles. Apostolate here, I think, means something like delegated authority. When we look at these three terms in their firstcentury context they add up to a combination of superintendence, authority and service. We are presented with a picture of a community in which the elders or rulers exercise their authority by being its servants, which is precisely what Jesus himself laid down as the correct way of organizing his community. 'He who would be chief among you shall be servant of all' (Mark 10.44).

In Acts 2 we have a description of what happened on the day of Pentecost: the coming of the gift of the Holy Spirit to the new community. The phenomena which fell upon the disciples caused a certain amount of unfavourable comment from the general public; some of them thought that the disciples were drunk. Peter felt it necessary to put them right on this matter, and he did so in a speech which divides into three distinct parts. The first runs from verses 14 to 21, the second from verses 22 to 28, and the third

from verses 29 to 36. The speech is marked by the occur‑
rence of direct vocatives. He begins in verse 14 by saying
'Men of Judaea and fellow Jews'. In verse 22 he starts
again, 'Fellow Israelites', and in verse 29 he says what is
usually translated 'Men and brethren'. I do not really know
how to translate *andres adelphoi*; the first word means just
'men' in general and the second means 'sharers of the same
faith and worship'.

The first part of the speech appeals to Scripture. The
things that have happened and the extraordinary mani‑
festations that have taken place are an indication that an
important prophecy in the Old Testament is being ful‑
filled, the prophecy from the Book of Joel (2.28–32). This
means that the Day of the Lord is at hand; consequently
the question of salvation or its opposite has become ex‑
tremely urgent.

The second part of the speech goes on to deal with
recent history and to link what has happened not only with
the Old Testament but also with the public career of Jesus.
It says in effect 'You may have thought that with the
crucifixion you were finished with Jesus for good and all,
but you are not. God has raised him from the dead and we
are here as witnesses of that, to testify to you concerning a
Messiah who has indeed been killed but has been raised
from the dead and is the effective force in all history from
now on.'

The third part of the speech links these events once more
with the old messianic hope and appeals to one of the
Psalms (16.10), which is taken to be a Psalm of David in
which he prophesied that he would not be left to lie in the
underworld but would have a better fate than that. 'But,'
says Peter, 'the fact is that David is in his grave, has been

for centuries and still is.' What he was prophesying about was not himself, but his descendant Jesus, and (verse 30) the crucial point is that David, who was in fact a prophet and knew that God had sworn by an oath that he would set someone physically descended from him upon his throne, spoke about the resurrection of the Messiah that 'he would neither be left in the abode of the dead nor would his flesh see corruption. And it was this Jesus that God raised up, and we are all witnesses of it. So he, having been raised to the right hand of God and having received the promise of the Holy Spirit from the Father, has poured out this, which you see and hear.' Verse 30 is the important verse; it expresses the expectation of the Messiah, a descendant of David who would be the ruler of God's people and seated on the throne of David.

There is a practical application of that argument in verses 37–42. As a result of what was said the hearers were impressed—deeply impressed—and they asked Peter and the others what they were to do. Peter said, 'Repent and be baptized in the name of Jesus Christ for the remission of your sins; and you will receive the gift of the Holy Spirit, for the promise is to you and your children and to all those who are far off, as many as the Lord our God shall call.' 'And with many other words he testified and exhorted them saying, "Save yourselves from this crooked generation".' 'Save yourselves from this crooked generation' is a reference to Deuteronomy (32.5). Peter exhorts God's people to separate themselves from their rebellious compatriots. A large number took this advice and were baptized, and about three thousand people were added to the church on that day. Acts 2.42 goes on to tell us that they were assiduous in attending on the teaching of the apostles and on the fellowship and the breaking of bread and the prayers.

This is the first picture in any kind of detail of what made up the life of the primitive Christian community and it is just as well to take a look at it as it stands. There is, first of all, the *teaching* of the apostles. Actually it is called the *didachē* of the apostles. Again our immediate reaction is to translate it into terms familiar to us and to think of a Bible Class of three thousand or the Annual Conference of the Society. But this will not do. We can see what this expression meant at the time because we have a little book called *The Didachē of the Twelve Apostles* which was discovered about eighty years ago. It was written in the second century and is a book of regulations for a Christian community. It starts off by describing two ways: the Way of Life and the Way of Death, and it lays down a lot of very sound principles regarding conduct, good and bad. Then it goes on to give detailed instruction about how the life of the community is to be carried on. In other words, the *Didachē* is a book of primitive Church law, the rules and regulations or constitution and bye-laws of the Christian community. It seems, then, that the apostles were regarded as custodians of the Law, the Christian *Torah* (and we have already seen that the Hebrew word *Torah*, which we commonly translate Law, really means instruction). The Community was under the guidance of the apostles.

The second word is the *Fellowship* (*Koinōnia*). It is not certain what it means. Fellowship is a very elastic term: it could mean any one of four things. It could mean fellowship with the apostles or association with them; it could mean fellowship in material possessions by sharing their things with one another (which we know from other state-

78

ments that in fact they did); or it could mean fellowship
with the community in general and particularly the fellowship of the common meal, the Christian common meal,
the 'breaking of bread' as it is sometimes called; or fourthly
it could mean charitable gifts, sharing their good things
with other people less fortunate. My own view of the
matter is that it probably means the practising of mutual
helpfulness and kindness. I am very much inclined to take
koinōnia in the sense of mutual kindness. In that case what
is there called *koinōnia* is in Simeon the Righteous called
'the imparting of kindnesses', the practice of mutual helpfulness as the expression of corporate solidarity.

The third thing referred to in verse 42 is the *breaking of
bread*. There are two important possibilities here. 'Breaking
of bread' could mean either an ordinary meal, or a ritual
observance involving the breaking and sharing of bread
and the eating of bread. Jeremias has pointed out that in
Jewish usage 'the breaking of bread' is not a normal expression for taking a normal meal,[1] so that we should
probably prefer to think of 'breaking of bread' as a ritual
meal. The rest of the evidence seems to bear this out. We
know that our Lord himself attached great importance to
certain ritual acts connected with the sharing of food. We
have an example in the accounts of the feeding of the
multitude, where we are told how he took bread, blessed it
and broke it. That was in fact the normal procedure for
saying grace according to Jewish custom, but it is more
than likely that Jesus had put more into the common meal
than ordinary Jewish practice did. That is to say that while
he said grace, as heads of Jewish households would say
grace, when he said it and shared out the food the meal

[1] J. Jeremias, *The Eucharistic Words of Jesus*, p. 83.

79

took on a special significance: it became a messianic meal. One of the ways in which the Jews pictured the golden age to come was as a great banquet, and it seems that underlying this meal of Jesus and the multitude was the idea that even if it was not a banquet in the proper sense, even if they could only share a crust of bread, it was a real messianic banquet in the sense that all the essentials of the messianic banquet were there. And that idea is carried over into the early Church.

The fourth element is the *prayers*. We will say more about this presently. When we go on from verse 42 to verses 44–46 we have a further description of the life of the believers, and again we are told four things about them. The first is that they were altogether: that is, I take it, that they formed a united group. I do not think it would be going too far to think that that group was united under the leadership of the Twelve. The second thing is that they 'had all things in common'. They sold real and personal property and divided it amongst all as anyone had need. That is, they pooled their resources. It is not necessary to go into the question whether this procedure was sound economics or not; doubtless it was not, but when people are expecting that the present age is going to be woundup any day they will not take very longterm views of economic questions. The third thing in verse 46 is that they were 'assiduous in one accord in the Temple' and that, I think, belongs with number four, the breaking of bread. If we letter the four elements in verse 42 thus:

(*a*) Teaching
(*b*) Fellowship
(*c*) Breaking of bread
(*d*) Prayers

and call the four elements in verses 44–46, 1, 2, 3, 4, then
1 corresponds to (*a*), 2 to (*b*), 3 to (*d*). Number 4 in verse 46
is the breaking of bread in private houses where they shared
their food in 'gladness and singleness (or generosity) of
heart, praising God and having favour with all the people';
this corresponds to (*c*).

Let us look further at this account. The prayers, that is
the worship, gives us the second item noted by Simeon the
Righteous.[1] So here we have the three pillars, the three
foundations, on which the world rests—the Law (instruction), the worship and the imparting of kindnesses. The
Law becomes the instruction of the apostles; the imparting
of kindnesses becomes the united fellowship and the pooling of resources; the worship becomes the prayers. The
worship Simeon had in mind was the worship of the
Temple, and it was to the Temple that the primitive
Christians went for worship. They did not go to the
synagogue, they went to the Temple. The breaking of
bread does not fit entirely into this picture, for the very good
reason that here we have something particularly Christian,
deriving from an action of Jesus right through his Ministry,
and done in a particularly marked way at the Last Supper.
If we want to bring it under one of these heads we should
have to bring it under 'worship', but it has also got something to do with the imparting of kindnesses.

We can now go further, and see these items appearing in
the narrative of the history of the primitive Church. In
Acts 3.1 we have prayers and worship. Peter and John are
on their way into the Temple at the hour of prayer, namely
the ninth hour, or 3 p.m. The prayers are connected with
the offering of the evening sacrifice. If we jump to Acts

[1] See above, p. 34.

4.32, we have 'And there was one mind and one soul among the multitude of believers', which is the same thing as is described by 'They were all together'. There was genuine unity of mind and spirit in the community, and that mind and spirit I take it came from the fact that they enjoyed a single guiding authority, that of the Twelve. 'And not one of them said that any of his possessions was his own, but all things were common to them'—that is, they sold private property and pooled their resources. 'And with great power the apostles witnessed to the resurrection of the Lord Jesus and great grace was upon them. For there was not a single person among them in want, for all who were possessors of lands or houses sold them and brought the proceeds of the things they had sold and laid them at the feet of the apostles and it was distributed to each according as anyone had need. And Joseph, who was surnamed Barnabas by the apostles (a name which means 'son of consolation') a Levite, a Cypriot by race (or family), to whom a field belonged (or a piece of land), sold it, brought the price and laid it at the feet of the apostles.' That is the Fellowship (*koinōnia*), the pooling of resources. Then in chapter 5 we have a further development of this theme, in the story of Ananias and Sapphira who sold some property but did not hand in the whole of the price, with disastrous consequences to themselves. Peter this time appears not only as giving instruction but also as a kind of judge passing sentence. In verse 12 we have a description of 'signs and wonders' wrought by the apostles, and it goes on to say that they were all in the porch or colonnade of Solomon. I assume this means that the cloister of the Temple was the regular meeting place of the community. That is natural enough. No private house would be big enough to hold an assembly of 3,000 people. If they were to meet anywhere they had probably got to meet in the open. And there again we have the unity, the 'altogether-ness', of the community.

In Acts 5.33–42 we have the account of how the Jewish authorities were displeased by the way in which the Christian community was growing and the steps they took to arrest its leaders. This produced a debate in the Sanhedrin as to what should be done with these people, and in the course of the debate the famous rabbinical teacher Gamaliel addressed the assembly. That is the Gamaliel who is claimed as the teacher of St Paul.[1] Gama-liel does not compare the Christian movement in Palestine to a curious Jewish sect, or an eccentric synagogue, or a hierarchical group. He compares it to the revolutionary movements of Theudas and Judas of Galilee. The picture that Gamaliel is represented as having before his mind's eye is the picture of a revolutionary community, not a queer sect of a religious character. It is as much political as reli-gious and, from Gamaliel's point of view, even more political than religious; and he says 'Let it alone.' Now if it were a matter of wrong theology or bad ethics I do not think that Gamaliel would have said 'Let it alone.' If he

[1] There has been a great deal of fuss about Gamaliel's speech; it is said that it could not have been made by him because one of the incidents which he speaks about did not occur at the relevant time. Theudas (to whom he refers in verse 36) made his insurrection in A.D. 44, and the speech of Gamaliel cannot be put as late as that. We are still quite near to the crucifixion, probably still in the early 30's. But that is not the point at the moment. Whether Gamaliel actually made this speech or whether somebody put it into his mouth, the point is that this is the kind of speech that either Gamaliel did in fact make or that would have been suitable for Gamaliel to make at this time. For our immediate purpose it does not matter which.

had thought of it as something which undermined the faith or the morals of Judah, something heretical in doctrine or immoral in practice by Jewish standards, he could not have tolerated it. But if it was thought of as a political movement, then he could say 'Let it alone, if God is behind it, it will prosper, if not it will perish'. I do not say that to regard it as a political movement is anything like the whole truth about the primitive Church, but it is a strong indication as to what it looked like to outsiders at that time.

If we turn to Acts 6.1-6, we have the appointment of deacons, and again we have got to clear our minds of modern notions. In my communion deacons are the people who take care of the collections, spend them to the best advantage and see that the buildings are kept in good repair. The first thing to notice about this passage is that the brethren are not in fact called deacons. 'Now in those days there came a complaint from the Christians of Jewish Greek origin against the native Hebrew Christians that their widows were overlooked in the daily ministration.' Something had gone wrong with the distribution, with the 'pooling of resources'. 'The Twelve called together the main body of the disciples and said to them, "It is not satisfactory that we should neglect the word of God in order to look after the rations" (serve tables, in other words), "therefore, brethren, seek out from your number seven men of good reputation, full of the Holy Spirit and wisdom, whom we will set over this task. As for us, we intend to apply ourselves strictly to prayer and the ministry of the word." And that proposition found favour with the entire gathering and they chose Stephen, a man full of faith and of the Holy Spirit, and Philip, and Prochorus, and

Nicanor, and Timon, and Parmenas, and Nicolas a proselyte of Antioch, and they presented them before the apostles and they prayed and laid their hands upon them.' They are not called deacons at all. They are the seven. The only place where they are mentioned again is in Acts 21.8, where they are called 'the Seven'. The title seems to be parallel to 'the Twelve'. This is quite clearly an organiza/tion for dealing with the *Koinōnia*, the sharing of the com/mon goods. I think it is possible that the ritual meal may also be involved though that is less certain.

When we put all this evidence together and ask ourselves what picture of the primitive Church it presents, I think we get something rather different from any religious organ/ization with which we are acquainted. It does not tally with anything that we know, from Roman Catholic to Baptist or Quaker. This is something which is like nothing but itself. In particular we must realize that the first com/munity that sprang up in Palestine as a result of the Ministry of Jesus was a community whose interests were as wide as the normal affairs of human life, and was not in the narrow sense religious at all. It was, in fact, an attempt to constitute the ideal Israel. Indeed one of the claims it made was that it *was* the New Israel. We have seen that Israel was something wider than just a worshipping com/munity: it was a community which included worship along with a whole range of other activities. My own guess would be that the only thing that differentiated the Christ/ian community from the surrounding Judaism so far as scope of interests were concerned was the fact that the Christian community was expecting the existing order to wind/up fairly soon and was therefore not likely to make any long/term programme on the economic side. The

Church in the first and second centuries was not just a worshipping society; like Judaism it was a community in a very much wider sense, it included worship, and many other things besides.

six

THE ORIGINAL TEACHING OF JESUS AND THE ETHICS OF THE EARLY CHURCH

W E have been studying the messianic community, the early Church, as a new kind of social organism. We have now to consider that this Church preserved a body of Jesus' teaching, and that from what was preserved it is possible for us to get adequate illumination for living in our own time. A good starting point is Mark 10.32–45. This sets out clearly the main issue that confronted Jesus and his followers in the course of his Ministry. 'They were on the way going up to Jerusalem, and Jesus was leading the way; and they were dumb-founded and those who followed were afraid. And taking again the Twelve he began to tell them the things that were going to happen, saying, "We are on our way to Jerusalem, and the Son of man will be betrayed to the chief priests and the scribes, and they will condemn him to death and hand him over to the gentiles, and they will mock him and spit on him and scourge him and kill him; and after three days he shall rise again".' That is a picture of the destiny of suffering and sacrifice that has been reserved for the Son of man.

Appended to it there is the story (beginning at verse 35) of the request of James and John. 'Master do for us what-ever we ask.' And he said, 'What do you want me to do for you?' And they replied, 'Grant us to sit in your glory.' That is, 'Allow us to sit in state with you, one on the left and one on the right.' Jesus replied, 'You do not know what you are asking. Are you able to drink the cup that I drink? or to be baptized with the baptism that I am baptized with?' And they said, 'We are able.' And Jesus said unto them, 'The cup that I drink ye shall drink; and with the baptism that I am baptized withal shall you be baptized; but to sit on my right hand or on my left hand is not mine to give: but it is for them for whom it has been prepared.' Now the Ten heard this, and they began to be annoyed with James and John (not because James and John wanted the chief places, but because they had jumped the queue!). Jesus called to them and said to them, 'You know that those who rule over the Gentiles lord it over them; and their great ones wield authority upon them. But it is not that way amongst you. On the contrary, whoever wishes to become great among you shall be your servant: and whoever would be first among you shall be servant of all. For the Son of man did not come to receive service but to give it, and to give his life a ransom for many.' We could not have a clearer statement of the contrasted hopes and ideals of Jesus and his contemporaries. Here side by side are two conceptions of the messianic task; one looks to the triumph and rule of the Messiah who sits on his throne and gives his orders; in the other there is a picture of the messianic Ministry in which the function of the Messiah is to be supremely the servant of all.

The messianic ideal cherished by Jesus is put by him in the form of a statement about the Son of man; the Ministry of which Jesus speaks is the Ministry of the Son of man; the sacrifice is the sacrifice of the Son of man. 'Son of man' is in one way an ambiguous term.[1] It means 'People of the saints of the Most High' (see Daniel 7), the people within Israel who are completely devoted to the worship and service of God, for whom the will of God is their supreme rule, who know no higher loyalty. But 'Son of man' can also be used as a name for the Messiah, in so far as the Messiah is himself the representative and embodiment of this 'People of the saints of the Most High'. The meaning can oscillate between the sacred community as a whole and its head, so that when it is said by Jesus that the Son of man must suffer that can mean—and probably does mean—either or both of two things. It can mean that the 'People of the saints of the Most High' must suffer, and it can mean that the Messiah must suffer. When it says that the Son of man must serve, it means that the 'People of the saints of the Most High' must serve and that the Messiah himself must serve. Jesus says to the sons of Zebedee, 'Can you drink the cup that I drink?' 'O yes, we can,' they reply. 'All right,' says Jesus, 'You will.' But when it comes to the point they did not; they all forsook him and fled, which is probably what most of us would have done in similar circumstances.

The Messiah says 'I do serve and I will suffer.' His acceptance of this challenge is found in two passages in Luke 22. The first is verses 24–27, which is Luke's version of the passage we have just considered in Mark. 'So now considerable contention developed among them as to who was the greatest. And he said to them, "The kings of the nations lord it over them and their men of authority are called benefactors. But you are not like that. The great man

[1] See T. W. Manson, *The Teaching of Jesus*, pp. 211–234, and *The Bulletin of John Rylands Library*, XXXII (1950), pp. 171–193.

among you let him become as the junior, and the leader as the servant. For who is greater, the diner or the waiter? You say the diner, but I say the waiter. I am among you as one giving service".' This passage does not only say that it is better to give service than to receive it; it makes the positive statement 'I am among you as a servant'.

Jesus' acceptance of the Messianic vocation of suffering occurs in the same chapter (verses 35–37). 'And he said to them, "When I sent you out without purse, wallet, or sandals, were you ever short of anything?" They said, "No." He said to them "It is different now; whoever has a purse had better take it and notes in a wallet too; and if anyone is short of a sword he had better sell his cloak and buy one. Why? Well, I can tell you that this text is about to have its fulfilment in me." ' Then Jesus quotes from Isaiah 53.12: 'he was reckoned among the lawless ones'; and he adds: 'For my career is coming to its close.' 'And they said, "Master, here are two swords"; and he said to them, "Well, well".' All this is very elusive, but the words allude to the tragedy of Jesus' ministry. The first part of the passage refers to a time of Jesus' popularity and acceptance, the second part is a very strong way of expressing the fact that they are now surrounded by enemies so ruthless that the possession of two swords will not help the situation. The messianic task can only be fulfilled in one way, and that the way indicated in the fifty-third chapter of Isaiah. This means that the Messiah must accept a destiny of suffering and death, as well as a task of service, which brings us back again to the passage in Mark about rules and the true test of greatness. When Jesus says 'Whoever would be great among you shall be your servant', he is not saying that those who are ambitious will be punished

by being compelled to do menial tasks, and *vice versa.*
Precise correspondences of that sort do not exist in the
messianic kingdom. In it greatness *is* service, and service *is*
greatness; no decoration is given for a life of service, the
life of service is the decoration.

The phrase in Mark 10.43, 'But it is not so among you',
has a history going back to the Old Testament, where we
find it translated 'It is not so done in Israel' (II Samuel
13.12) to describe conduct that is incompatible with being
the People of God. So the Christian ethic has its first
acceptance within the Christian community. It is 'done'
or 'not done' among 'you'. From there it may spread to the
outside world, but if it does not begin there it is not likely
to begin anywhere. But if the Christian ethic begins within
the Christian fellowship it cannot stay there: the service and
sacrifice of Christ are 'for many' (Mark 10.45; 14.24).
Jeremias has shown that 'many' in these verses has an
inclusive meaning; it is a way of saying that the Son of man
who 'gave his life a ransom for many' is really giving his
life for the common good.[1] There is an interesting parallel
to this statement in the words of institution at the Last
Supper: 'He said to them, "This is my covenant blood,
which is shed for many"' (Mark 14.22). Again it means
for the general good. It follows that as the Messiah sacri-
ficed himself for the common good, so the community or
people of the saints of the Most High must be expendable
also for the common good.

It was not very easy for the early Church to accept this in
its full meaning and with all its practical implications. It
was no easier for it than it is for us. Even when it had got
away from the idea of a messianic triumph and the shaping

[1] See J. Jeremias, *The Eucharistic Words of Jesus*, pp. 148 ff.

of an Israelite world empire, there was still the standing temptation for the Christian community to become a 'saved Remnant' rather than a 'saving Remnant',[1] to think of themselves as elected for privilege rather than for service, and so to make the words and deeds of Jesus the standard and pattern of their internal discipline rather than the inspiration of an apostolic mission.

When we read the Acts of the Apostles it would seem as if the apostolic or missionary task was forced upon the primitive Church. What really started its missionary work was the persecution that followed the martyrdom of Stephen (Acts 8.1). Another factor that set the missionary work going was the outburst of missionary zeal that took place in Antioch (Acts 13). This outburst does not appear to have been initiated by any influence from Jerusalem: the entire credit is given to the Holy Spirit poured out on the community at Antioch. It is probably only when Paul went up to Jerusalem and started talking about foreign missions to the leaders of the Jerusalem Church that they decided to make some arrangements for carrying them on.

On the other hand the narrowness of outlook at the beginning of the primitive Church, chiefly concerned with shaping itself as an elect body separated from the surround-ing wickedness, has its good side. If the primitive Church tended to keep Jesus to itself, at least it did take him seri-ously. One of the ways in which it did so was by turning his teaching inwards upon itself. If we think in terms of strict historical documentation these early Christians were guilty of tampering with the evidence. But they did not regard themselves as bound to store up archives for the

[1] Cf. T. W. Manson, *The Teaching of Jesus*, p. 179.

investigation of historians nineteen centuries later. They saw themselves as the messianic community, and the words of Jesus their Master as full of instruction for them. They were prepared to take his sayings and apply them to their own case, and if in the process sayings which had originally been intended to serve other purposes were diverted, that did not appear to them to be a serious matter. This process has lately been made the subject of close and detailed study by C. H. Dodd[1] and J. Jeremias,[2] and in what follows I am making a good deal of use of what they have to say.

We can see the process at work most clearly in the case of the parabolic teaching of Jesus. Every authentic parable had originally its own actual situation in the life of Jesus. There was a day, a set of circumstances, and a definite group of people; and it was on that day, in those circumstances and to those people that the parable was first uttered. But not every parable has succeeded in keeping its original context. By the time they have been included in the Gospel, many have been given a new situation in the life of the early Church. Once we have got over the shock of realizing that the parables have been treated in this way to meet new situations, the fact is encouraging rather than otherwise, because it really means that the men of the early Church did not normally invent sayings of Jesus to express their own convictions, but rather that they selected from the mass what they thought was relevant. Admittedly the chosen words of Jesus may have been misunderstood or made to speak to a new situation in ways not originally intended by Jesus. The early Church remembered better than it under-stood. This means that the better we understand the mind

[1] *Parables of the Kingdom*, chapter 4.
[2] *The Parables of Jesus*, pp. 20–38.

93

of the early Church, the more likely it is that we shall be able to reverse the process that went on in the first decades, to strip off mistaken interpretations and applications and see the utterances in their original intention. We may not be able to reconstruct the actual situation, but we should be able readily to conceive the kind of situation in which it would be very much to the point.

This process of adaptation of the sayings of Jesus has two important characteristics. One is that the audience to which the saying or parable is addressed is changed. It is possible to go through the sayings of Jesus classifying them accord/ing to their audience—disciples, opponents or the general public. One fact that emerges when one goes into this in detail is that some of the sayings that appear in more than one Gospel are addressed to opponents in one and to disciples in another. There is evidence of a tendency to transfer sayings originally spoken to opponents to dis/ciples; but there is no evidence of traffic in the other direction, of sayings originally spoken to disciples being re/addressed to people outside. Now why does this change take place? What is it that makes the tradition turn polemical utterance designed for outsiders into exhortations addressed to members of the community? I suggest that it is tied up with the fact that the primitive Palestinian community thought of itself as a kind of Israel within Israel; that it thought of itself as receiving a new Law from Jesus, and of Jesus as a new Moses (cf. Deuteronomy 18.15 ff.). Given a community of this kind, which thought of itself as Israel within Israel receiving Law from its messianic prophet, the oracles of that messianic prophet would all be precious, and the more precious where they could be understood as legislation for the community. That some of these oracles had been spoken in the first instance to those outside did not matter very much. Those outside had rejected the new Law in much the same way that the nations of the world had rejected the Law of Moses. The Christian community accepted and claimed the new revelation as Israel had accepted and claimed the old. Thus we are witnesses of a process by which the day-to-day answers of Jesus, his ways of dealing with the particular concrete situations that arose during his Ministry, are turned into the laws and customs of the Church. It is significant for the general question of the reliability of the Gospels as historical documents that it is the absorption and adaptation of existing material and not the creation of new material, with which we are presented.

The second element in the process of adaptation is the turning of teaching which was eschatological in its intention and very often threatening in its meaning into exhortations and ethical advice for the community. The solemn warning to the outsider becomes wise counsel to the church member or the church leader. That is illustrated in a very striking way by a short parable in Matthew 5.25.[1] There, in the context of the Sermon on the Mount and in a general passage dealing with the necessity of having a conciliatory and friendly attitude to one's neighbour, Christian disciples are told to come to terms with the adversary quickly while they are still with him on the way to the court, in case the adversary delivers them to the judge and the judge to the prison-keeper and they are thrown into prison, where they will be kept until the last farthing is paid. Here the parable shows the Christian community the necessity of being reconciled to its neighbours and being on decent terms with

[1] Previously referred to above, p. 47.

them. But when we turn to the parallel passage in Luke (12.54 ff.) it is a very different story. Now it is addressed to the crowd, the general public. 'He said to the crowd, "When you see a cloud rising in the west you say, 'We shall have rain'; and when you observe the east wind blowing you say, 'There will be a heat-wave'. And so it is. Hypocrites, you know how to interpret the phenomena of the earth and sky; why can you not interpret this present situation? You can judge the seasons; why do you not judge what is right by yourselves? For as you are on your way with your adversary to the court take the opportunity to be quit of him." ' Here the hearers are asked to consider the gravity of the times and the need to 'get right with God' while there is still time. What has happened is that the urgent and very necessary warning to outsiders in Luke has been adapted in Matthew to meet the needs of a Church whose members are not in need of any such warning because they *have* come to terms with God. The parable is now used as an exhortation to Christians to be conciliatory and to come to an agreement with their neighbours.

Another example can be taken from Luke (16.1–13), where we have the story of the 'Dishonest Steward' who was accused by his master of embezzlement and falsifying the accounts. The master orders an immediate audit, and the steward realizes he is likely to lose his job, so he sets to work with people owing money to his master and hopes to establish them as friends who will take care of him when he is out of work. This parable has always caused a lot of uneasiness to Christians because of verse 8, 'And the master commended the unrighteous steward because he had done wisely'. It looks as if Jesus is commending shabby tricks. But the fact that Jesus applauded his cunning does not mean he approved of the man. The steward was a scoundrel, but a pretty smart scoundrel all the same. Let the children of light be equally alert! There follows (from verse 9) a number of commands in the mouth of Jesus himself. 'I say to you, Make yourselves friends by means of the mammon of unrighteousness; when it runs out they may receive you into everlasting dwellings. Men reliable in the smallest matters will be reliable in big things. He who is dishonest in small matters will be dishonest in big.' Then there is another detached reflection: 'If you have not turned out faithful or reliable in the unrighteous world; if you have not been reliable with other people's goods, who would give you your own?' 'No servant can serve two masters, for either he will hate the one and love the other; or else he will stick to one and despise the other. You cannot serve God and mammon.' All these give the impression of being detached sayings that have been linked to this parable because of something to do with reliability, or with the question of serving one master or several. The original force of the parable has nothing to do with the morals of the steward. This dishonest steward—dishonest to begin with and dishonest to the end—finds himself in a fix, and being in a fix he takes steps to get himself out of it. Granted that the steps he took were as dishonest as the steps that had brought him into the fix, but he did take energetic action to get out once he was in. The primary intention of the parable is to say to people in the world at large, 'You also are in a fix and the evil day for you is not very far away. If you had any sense you would take steps, and urgent steps, to get yourselves out of the fix while there is still time.' In other words, the dishonest steward and the man on the way to the law court are in origin similar cases, but when the early Church adopted them they also adapted them for a community which had already made its peace with God, and therefore had to apply them in some way to fit its own situation.

The parable of the labourers in the vineyard (Matthew 20.1–16) is another example of what appears to be change of audience. Here again is a parable which has worried a lot of good people, who feel a certain sympathy with the men who worked all day and at the end got no more than those who had laboured only for the last hour. But this is to miss the point. The essential meaning of the parable is in verse 15, 'Or is your eye evil, because I am good?' Everybody got the basic minimum wage, one *denarius* per day, which was just enough to keep a working man and his family, and no more. The people who worked the full day got the full day's pay; to give the people who had worked less than the full day something less than the day's pay would be to inflict hardship on them, because the one *denarius* was the minimum wage. The force of the parable is to emphasize the goodness, the kindness, of the employer who gives the one group of workers what they are entitled to, and to the others what they are not entitled to but what, in fact, they need.

The parallel to these workers is the case of the two brothers in the parable of the 'Prodigal Son' (Luke 15. 11–32). There the party is open to both brothers, they are both entitled to come in and have a plate of veal and stuffing and everything else that is provided. The trouble is that the elder brother is not content: he either wants more himself or the prodigal to have less; this kind of equality of treatment irks him. It is probable that the parable ends with a rebuke to the scribes and the pharisees who wanted God to discriminate. They wanted the undeserving to get less. They did not want 'parties for prodigals'. What the prodigal should get is a good plain suit of clothes, a good plain diet and plenty of work: discipline would be good for him. But God does not measure or discriminate in that way. When the parable came to be used in the early Church it was a community where some worked harder for it than others, and the parable became a warning to such folk that they must not expect special consideration because they had been particularly loyal; even the Twelve should not expect a lot of extras. In any case one is not dealing here with things that can be weighed and measured: one is dealing with the love of God, which cannot be divided up into parcels of different sizes for different people.

A further example of a change of audience is found earlier in the same chapter, the parable of the man who has a hundred sheep and loses one, and goes to seek the lost one and does not rest until he has got it back (Luke 15.3–7). In Luke this is addressed to the pharisees and scribes and is a rebuke to them for criticizing the way in which Jesus deals with publicans and sinners and is so friendly with them. In Matthew, however, it appears in a different context (18.12–14). Here it is in an address to the disciples concerned with the internal organization and discipline of the Christian community, and it has become a warning to those within the Church not to be harsh and censorious to their brothers. An original rebuke against a harsh attitude towards people *outside* the Christian community has now become an exhortation to preserve a spirit of kindness and brotherly love *within* it.

It is possible to go on multiplying examples. Take, for instance, the parable of the 'Great Feast' (Matthew 22.1–10;

Luke 14.16–24). In its original setting in the ministry of
Jesus the parable was a reproach to his contemporaries for
their unwillingness to accept what was being offered to
them; a reproach for their refusal to enter the kingdom of
God when the doors were standing wide open. As it now
stands in the Gospels we can see it has been turned into
encouragement to missionary effort on the part of the
Christian community. The emphasis is now on the idea of
going out to bring people in. It is interesting to see that in
Matthew the instructions to the servants are to make only
one expedition 'into the streets and lanes of the city'. In
Luke there are two expeditions, one 'into the streets and
lanes' and the other 'into the highways and hedges', in the
country. It is quite possible that that extra expedition has in
mind the expansion of the Christian community beyond
Judaea to the Gentiles.

Again there is the picture of the thief in the night
(Matthew 24.43 ff.; Luke 12.39 ff.). If the householder
had known what time the thief would come he would have
been watching. This was originally intended as an appeal
to those outside the group of followers of Jesus to realize the
urgency of the times and to take steps to deal with the
situation. Jesus says, in effect, to his contemporaries, 'You
are living on the edge of a volcano and it is urgent that you
should do something about it before it erupts on you.' By
the time the Church took it over it had become a warning
to church members and leaders to be watchful and alert
because at any moment the second coming may take place.
The parable of the ten virgins (Matthew 25.1–13) is a
warning to outsiders by Jesus that a crisis is at hand, but
as applied in the life of the Church it is an exhortation
to church members to be prepared and equipped. The

original setting of the parable of the doorkeeper (Mark 13. 33–37; Luke 12.35–38) was a warning to the leaders of the Jewish community that the crisis of the coming kingdom is at hand, and that they are neglecting their duty if they do not see it coming and help their fellow countrymen to appreciate the urgency of the matter. But in the Christian community it becomes an exhortation to church members and church leaders not to become lax because the second coming is delayed. The same may be said about the parable of the pounds (Matthew 25.14–30; Luke 19.12–27).

It is important to realize what has happened. While Jesus was going about his own ministry he often reproached his hearers because they had the wrong attitude to God and to their fellow men, and tried to bring them to a different attitude. That situation had passed and a new one had taken its place, a situation in which Jesus had already suffered and died and risen. The Christian community was now trying to learn from his sayings and doings, and they took them and found ways of applying what had been said, for example to scribes and pharisees, to their own case. It is arguable that they misunderstood a great deal of what they adapted. No doubt they did. I have already said that there is very little doubt that they remembered far better than they understood. The point is that they *did* remember, and they *did* try to understand. Because they did these two things they preserved for us the chance of understanding more fully and of having a clearer picture of these words and deeds of Jesus which are a standing inspiration and challenge, and as often as not a standing rebuke, to us all. They could not have done it if they had not taken these words and deeds of Jesus with complete seriousness and accepted them as applicable to themselves. This is a striking contrast to the attitude which sees how well a rebuke applies to someone else, or how pointed advice is for someone else, but does not accept it for onself. We can give the early Church full marks for diverting the rebukes that were given to outsiders and asking itself 'where does that touch me?'

We have come to the end of our study, and the points that I would like to stress are few but important. The first is that the ethic we are dealing with is the ethic of a king, dom: the ethic of a society with a leader and ruler; and the primary quality of the ethic is that it comes from the ruler himself, who is the interpreter and exemplifier of it. This holds if we think in terms of the kingdom of God, in which God himself gives the rules of life and exemplifies them; 'you are to be holy as God is holy; perfect as he is perfect; merciful as he is merciful.' It still holds if we think of it in the terms of a messianic kingdom. It is the Messiah whose life and death exemplifies and interprets the ideal which is summed up in the commandment 'Love as I have loved you'. In the last resort the Christian ethic inevitably comes back to Christ himself. It is from him that it derives its content, its form and its authority. Its force is most likely to be felt by those who belong to the community which he founded and maintains, the community which belongs to him. And the power to carry it into effect is most likely to be found in living association with that community and with its head.

If the Christian ethic is anything at all it is a living, growing thing. 'Love as I have loved you' is not to be construed solely in the past; if there is anything in the Christian religion 'I have loved you' is true of the past, the present, and the future. 'I *have* loved', in the perfect tense, means that it is a past thing which continues into the present until the end of time. Further, just as the power and inspiration of the Christian ethic is represented in a living person and a living body, so the achievement of Christian ethics is always something new and original. Christian ethics is certainly not a slavish obedience to rules and regu⁄lations. It is active living, and therefore it has the power to go to the heart of every ethical situation as it arises. It has the power to see what response is called for in terms of feeling, word and act, and the power to make that response, and make it creatively and effectively. In short, Christian ethics is a work of art.

INDEX OF BIBLICAL REFERENCES

Genesis
2.23   16
29.14   16

Exodus
20.2   19

Leviticus
11.44 f.   19
19.2   19, 58
19.18   61
20.7   19
20.26   19

Numbers
15.37–41   33
15.40 f.   19

Deuteronomy
ch. 4   20
5.1   20
6.3   20
6.4   61
6.4–9   33
11.13–21   33
18.15 ff.   94
32.5   77

Judges
9.2 f.   16

II Samuel
5.1   16
chs. 11–12   26
13.12   91

15.1–4   23
ch. 24   26

I Kings
3.16–27   23
8.22–53   24
12.16   23
14.8   25
ch. 22   26

II Kings
21.2, 9   25
22.2   25

Job
ch. 28   31

Psalms
16.3   19
16.10   76
19.7–11   29
34.10   19
119.97–104   30

Proverbs
chs. 8 and 9   31
8.22–31   31

Isaiah
ch. 53   90
53.12   90

Daniel
ch. 7   89
8.24   19

Hosea
1.4   16
1.6   16
1.9   16
2.21–23   16

Joel
2.28–32   76

Micah
6.8   18

Ecclesiasticus
15.1   31
19.20   31
21.11   31
24.7–12   31
34.8   31

Matthew
ch. 5   47
5.1 f.   50
5.3–12   51
5.13–16   51
5.17 f.   53
5.17–48   52 f.
5.25 f.   47, 95
5.48   19
ch. 6   47
6.1–34   52, 54 ff.
6.2–4   55
6.16   55
6.19–21   55

6.22 f.	55	ch. 4	45	2.22	76	
6.24	55	6.36	19	2.22–28	75	
6.25–34	56	7.34	56	2.29	76	
ch. 7	56	11.20	48	2.29–36	76	
7.1–12	52	12.35–38	101	2.30	77	
7.13–29	56 f.	12.39 ff.	100	2.37–42	77	
16.18	69	12.54 ff.	96	2.42	77, 80	
18.12–14	99	12.57 ff.	47	2.44–46	80, 81	
18.17	69	14.16–24	100	2.46	80, 81	
19.21	59	15.3–7	99	3.1	81	
19.28	74	15.11–32	98	3.12–26	72	
20.1–16	98	15.17	65	4.8–12	72	
20.15	98	15.21	64	4.32	82	
20.20–28	59	16.1–13	96 f.	ch. 5	82	
22.1–10	99 f.	16.8	96	5.12	82	
22.40	61	18.9	56	5.33–42	83	
24.43 ff.	100	19.12–27	101	5.38	83	
25.1–13	100	22.24–27	89 f.	6.1–6	84	
25.14–30	101	22.29–30	74	8.1	92	
28.20	68	22.35–37	90	12.2	74	
				ch. 13	92	
Mark				21.8	85	
10.21	55	*John*				
10.32–45	87 ff.	13.15	62			
10.35–45	58	13.34	62	*Galatians*		
10.43	91	15.12	62	2.20	63	
10.44	75			chs. 5–6	21	
10.45	91					
12.28–34	60	*Acts*		*Ephesians*		
13.33–37	101	1.15–22	72	chs. 1–3	21	
14.22	91	1.20	75	chs. 4–6	21	
14.24	91	1.25	75			
		ch. 2	75	*I Peter*		
Luke		2.14	76	1.1–2.10	21	
1.74 ff.	25	2.14–21	75	2.11–5.11	21	
		2.14–36	72			

GENERAL INDEX

Ananias, 82
Aqiba, rabbi, 31
Aristotle, 12 f.
Athens, civilization of, 15

Barnabas, 82
Bartlett, Vernon, 73
Baxter, Richard, 59 f.
Beatitudes, 51
Bishops, 75
Body of Christ, the, ch. 5 *passim*
Breaking of bread, 79 f., 81
Burnet, John, 12 f.
Butler, B. C., 49

Christian community, the, ch. 5
    passim, ch. 6 *passim*
Church, the, ch. 5 *passim*, ch. 6
    passim
Cook, S. A., 22
Covenant, 18, 38, 53 f.
Covenanters of Damascus, 72

Danby, H., 31, 34, 52
David, 23, 25, 26
Dead Sea Scrolls, 72
Deuteronomy, code of, 19 f.
Diaconate, 75, 84
Dibelius, M., 46 ff.
Didache, 78
Dodd, C. H., 93
Doughty, C. M., 22

Ecclēsia, 70 f.
Ecclesiasticus, 31
Essenes, community of, 71

Farewell Discourses in St John's
    Gospel, 62, 65
Fellowship, 78 f., 80, 82
Finkelstein, L., 35
Following Christ, ch. 4 *passim*
Friedlander, Gerald, 57

Gamaliel, 83
Greek approach to ethics, 12 ff.

Hebrew and Greek ways of think-
    ing, 14 ff., 35
Herod Agrippa, 74
Ḥesed, 37
Hippolytus, 70

Ibn Saud, 22, 24
Israel, prophets of, 24
    relation between God and, 18 ff.
    the New, ch. 5 *passim*

James the son of Zebedee, 74
Jeremias, J., 79, 91, 93
Jesus
    and the Law of Moses, ch. 3
        passim
    and the New Law, ch. 3 *passim*,
        58

Jesus, original teaching of, ch. 6 *passim*
Josephus, 71
Judaism, ch. 1 *passim*, ch. 2 *passim*, 52 f., 63 f.
Judas of Galilee, 83
Judas Iscariot, 74

Kāhāl, 70 f.
Kahle, P., 71
Kawwānāh, 39 f., 42, 43, 63
'Kindnesses,' imparting of, 37, 38, 39, 52, 79, 81
Kingdom of God, 28, 34, 52, 65, 67, 102
Kingship, of God, 21, 65, 67
Semitic or Hebrew concept of, 21 ff., 28, 65, 67
Koinōnia, 78 f., 82, 85

Law, 28 ff., 43 ff., 65, 81, 94 f.
Hebrew, ch. 2 *passim*, 43 ff., 61
Roman, 35
Lawrence, T. H., 22
Legalism, 66
Lishmāh, 41 f., 43, 63
Loewe, H., 33, 40, 41, 42
Lovingkindness, 37 f.

Marcion, 44
Matthias, 75
Mercy, 37 f.
Messianic ideal, the, 88 ff.
Ministry, the, 88 f.
Mishnāh, 31, 34, 43, 74
Monotheism, 35
Greek, 35

Hebrew, 35, 44 ff.
Montefiore, C. G., 33, 40, 41, 42
Moore, G. F., 41
Moses, 29, 34
Law of, ch. 2 *passim*, ch. 3 *passim*, 95

Neighbour, right relations with, 61 ff.
New Testament, 20 f., ch. 3 *passim*
Nicanor, 85
Nicolas, 85
Nomos, 28

Old Testament, ch. 1 *passim*, ch. 2 *passim*
code of conduct, 19 f., 43 ff.

Parables, the, 93 ff.
Parmenas, 85
Paul, 83, 92
Pedersen, J., 22
Pentateuch, 20, 35, 36
People of God, 71
Perfection, 59
Pirkē Aboth, 31, 34, 52
Plato, 12 ff.
Philo, 71
Prayers, 80
Prochorus, 84
Property, 80, 82

Rabbinical sayings, 40 f.
Remnant, the, 92
Rights, 38
of personality, 35
of property, 35

General Index

Robertson, F. W., 62
Robinson, H. A. Wheeler, 26

Sapphira, 82
Saul, 23, 26
Self-realization, ethic of, 64
Sermon on the Mount, 45 ff., 65,
66, 95
Shĕma', 32 f., 61
Simeon the Righteous, 34 ff., 52,
79, 81
Smith, W. Robertson, 22
Solomon, 23, 24
Stark, Freya, 22
Stephen, 84, 92

Talmûd, 43
Teaching of the apostles, 78, 80

Ten Commandments, 19, 20, 35
Therapeutae, 71, 72
Theudas, 83
Timon, 85
Torah, 27, 28, 29, 30, 31, 52, 78
Tovey, Sir Donald, 66 ff.

Windisch, H., 50
Wisdom, 31
of God, 31
of Solomon, 31
Worship, 36, 39, 52, 54 f., 81, 85 f.
of the synagogue, 36, 54
private, 36
in New Testament times, 36
Israelite attitude to, 36 f.
modern attitude to, 37